for my good friends –
Paul 12-16

BEACH GUIDE
TO
Marie-Galante

The Emerald World
Where Time Has Stopped

PAUL J. SAUSVILLE

Feuillere Beach

⤳ *Picture a place...* ⤳

where a warm tropical breeze softly sweeps the sweet bouquet of tropical flowers over the land. Small town values of trust and friendship guide the lives of islanders. Children play freely throughout the villages without fear of crime. Everyone looks after neighbors. Time passes slowly. Each breath is savored for the gift that it is.

On this "Goldilocks" island everything is "just right." There are powder-white beaches, coconut palm trees and intimate lagoons of emerald green. The islanders live a life of simple pleasures, as if time had stopped long, long ago.

Does such a place really exist you may ask? Why, yes it does. It is a small island, located twenty miles off the shores of Guadeloupe. It is the island of Marie-Galante.

This book describes in detail the 12 beautiful beaches of Marie-Galante; how to find them, which beaches are best for sunsets, moonrises, snorkeling, surfing, hiking and swimming and how to enjoy them as well as the charm of the island itself. It is a one-of-a-kind beach guide.

If you are looking for calm and beautiful paradise beaches you will want to learn more about Marie-Galante, the emerald world where time has stopped.

ABOUT THE AUTHOR

The "Beach Guide to Marie-Galante – The Emerald World Where Time Has Stopped" is from the works of Paul J. Sausville, professional engineer, consultant and environmental scientist. His research and mathematical models have led to the clean-up of New York's waters. As a legislator and public official he crafted environmental laws and public policies for State and local government.

Paul traveled throughout the Caribbean in search of paradise – a magical island free of hurried tourists, where each day is – as the day before – sunny, warm, peaceful and beautiful. That island is called Marie-Galante.

All inquiries should be directed to the author:

Beach Guide c/o
Paul J. Sausville
1074 Raymond Road
Malta, New York 12020
518-885-4533

Book Design and Graphic Artwork:
Linda Ramsey, ramseygraphicdesign@gmail.com

ISBN Number: 978-0-692-68633-1
Library of Congress Control Number: 2016905822
Website: BeachGuide.website

First Printing 2016

ACKNOWLEDGEMENTS

This book is a collaborative effort of many people who have helped to make it a success. Thanks to the following for their contributions of photos, insights, research and editing.

Thanks to the tourist offices at Marie-Galante and the Guadeloupe Islands Tourist Board, especially Claudia Lengrat and Michel Kozminski both of whom helped me bridge the French/American culture. We shared a common goal of reporting to the world the discovery of paradise, Marie-Galante.

Thanks to my island friends and coaches Jean-Michel Dufour, Cedwin Schmitt of Pegases Creations, Stella and Richard Ardens and the many island business leaders who shared with me local insights. A special thanks to my angel Alison Rosinel who not only provided photos for the book but also introduced me to the soul of the island.

Thanks to my proof reading and editing friends - my wife Nancy, Pat Carlton, Ruth Shiebler, Lois Mitchell, Steve Sanborn and Terry Hoffman. They spent countless hours editing the manuscript and making suggestions for improvement. They found errors in early drafts and more errors in successive drafts as the book progressed to completion. Thanks to the genius of Linda Ramsey of Ramsey Graphic Design who did a fantastic job of layout.

Others who advised and contributed to the development of this project include Ray O'Connor, Abbey Frederick, Gerry McMullen, Professor Richard Ryan, Professor Charlene Grant and Dr. Grant Cornwell.

Thanks to the professionals at the National Oceanic and Atmospheric Administration (NOAA) and the US Fish & Wildlife Service. Their research and photos explain the importance of protecting the special environment that blesses life here on Earth.

In the course of writing this book I have reviewed countless websites and books and taken a bit from each. I don't know how much of this book contains information from these resources, surely most of it. Where it has been possible to quote these sources I have done so; where not, you may recognize your work. My gratitude to you for your contribution. You have made a difference.

PHOTO CREDITS

Photos were taken by the author or were contributed by the tourist boards of Marie-Galante and Guadeloupe Islands (Photos©JadDavenport/Guadeloupe Islands Tourism Board – 2015)

The following are credits for other photos used in the book.

Rip Current, Parrotfish, Sea Fan, Coral and Sponge, Reef Fish, Netted Turtle: and Hawksbill Turtle Courtesy: National Marine Fishery Services of National Oceanic and Atmospheric Administration (NOAA) and US Fish & Wildlife Service

Plunging Wave: Pixabay

Treasure (Ring): Gerry McMullen

Topographic Maps: IGN of France

Rain Cloud, Very Special Island: Alison Rosinel Photography

Moonrise: Guillarmo Gomez Gil, Bridgeman Art Gallery

Sunset: Bynnsha Photography

Hawksbill Turtle: US Fish and Wildlife Service

Stupendemys: Wikimedia

Explorer Ship: Valentin Schwind

Ayaycia: Courtesy of Coka/Photokore and Dreamstime.com

Aerial View Mays Beach:'robertharding / Alamy

Stupendemys Turtle:Wikimedia

Urchin: Courtesy of Michael Wolf and commons.wikimediia.org

Turtle Watermark Artwork: J. C. ParkerFineArt.com

FORWARD

"The simple secret of happiness is a simple life"
Mehmet Murat ildan

The sun was going down as we stepped off the ferry and onto the dock at the small village of Grand-Bourg in the remote Caribbean island of Marie-Galante. Signs were held up to unite new guests with their hosts. Taxis and cars were departing--- to home for commuters and to cottages and villas for tourists. In ten minutes the ferry dock was empty, that is except for my wife Nancy and me.

We had expected to see a welcoming sign with our names on it, as we had never been to the island before and had not met our villa host. We waited. As we later found out, our host, Silvie, was expecting us to arrive the following day.

So, here we were on the shores of this remote tropical island in the French West Indies. We didn't speak French and our greeter who was to drive us to the dream villa that we had rented 6 months earlier was not at the dock.

Snow storms in upstate New York had resulted in flight cancellations that forced us into last minute plans that took us through a two-day travel experience to Washington, DC, Miami and San Juan for an overnight stay. Then came a next day flight to Guadeloupe, followed by a 1 hour ferry ride to this end-of-the-earth paradise island. Connections had gone smoothly -- up until now. You can imagine the anxiety and sense of helplessness we felt after 2 days of airport life.

I don't remember just how we met our angel (a local man on a bicycle who didn't speak English) but he stopped and spoke to us in words that we didn't understand. While he hadn't planned to assist strangers that evening, he stopped and offered us his assistance. After reading the email message written in French he pulled a cell phone from his pocket and dialed. In Marie-Galante everyone knows and cares about each other. ***Our angel on a bike knew Silvie.***

In a few minutes Silvie was at the dock profusely apologetic (at least she sounded apologetic as she spoke only French). With her was Alison an outgoing young woman who spoke English and could help us with the car rental and lead us to our villa.

At the villa we talked with Alison and Silvie and met Silvie's children who were interested in looking at us and hearing us speak English, as if we were visitors from the moon. Alison, Silvie and the children were with us for an hour, answering our questions and introducing us to the culture of Marie-Galante. And with a great offering of kindness, they were to return throughout our two-week

vacation to offer advice and assistance. During this time, we met many other island people who helped us with the language of French, always willing and with an understanding smile.

As we came to know the people living in Marie-Galante we learned they are as pure, kind and as beautiful as the island itself. They enjoy the simple pleasures of life, making a living on an economy that relies mostly on tourism, fishing and farming.

And so throughout this book I will talk about the sparkling beauty of Marie-Galante's beaches, but it is the people who are the real jewels of this precious island.

I have some concern about writing this book for fear that it will in some small way change Marie-Galante. Should I bear any responsibility for this, I apologize. My hope is that the world outside of Marie-Galante will be a better place by getting to know her and the charming people who live there.

It is a great honor to dedicate this book to the friendly people of Marie-Galante, especially to Silvie, Alison and to their families who call our name as we pass their homes. We had found, "The Emerald World Where Time Has Stopped."

Paul J. Sausville

CONTENTS

INTRODUCTION

*I know where I want to be- and it's here, where life comes
full to me with every wash of the waves.*
Richard Bode, Beachcombing at Miramar

In a sea far, far away lies a magical place, a little known island lost among the 7000 islands of the Caribbean Sea. Overhead each day a warm sun awakens life and each night the moon and stars a million-fold in the heavens above sparkle in the darkness. On the shores are white sandy beaches of coral, emerald lagoons and palm trees swaying in the tropical breeze. Birds sing in the trees, cattle low in the meadow and waves lap on the beaches. These are the sounds of this paradise island.

Life abounds. Gardens, flowers and the grasses in the meadow are nourished by the mist of a gentle rain shower that passes by each day. Beauty is everywhere to be seen. All you have to do is look.

Islanders live in the moment, breathing each moment as if it might be their last. They live in peace with family, friends and neighbors.

It is a real island, located twenty miles off the shores of Guadeloupe. It is the island of Marie-Galante.

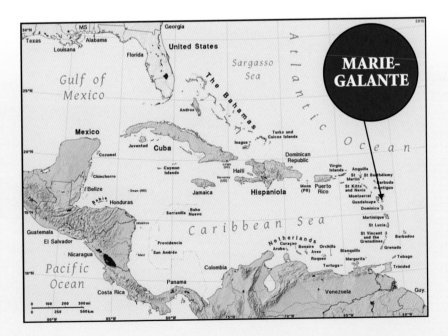

The island was called *Aichi* by the Caribs and *Touloukaera* by the Arawaks. Today it is "l'île de belles personnes" - the island of beautiful people.

It is an island undiscovered; home to some of the most beautiful and deserted beaches in the world. Small farms of sugarcane cover the land from horizon to horizon. Fields are harvested "Amish-like" with the hands of hardworking farmers using machetes and dual oxen-drawn carts, methods of another time. The island lifestyle is one that most people dream of and few can believe actually exists. Here, life slows down, the mood of life changes and time stops. For the islanders, each day is beautiful. They carry happiness within.

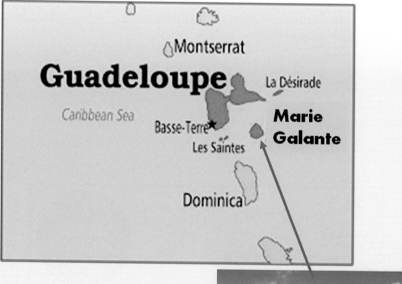

After first visiting Marie-Galante, I decided to return to discover her secrets and record the magic, extreme beauty and special tranquility of the quiet beaches that few people know of and understand.

· · · · · · · · · · · · · · · · · · · ·

Happiness is ... not in another place but in this place,
not in another hour but in this hour.

Walt Whitman

· · · · · · · · · · · · · · · · · · · ·

This book is not only a guide to these heavenly beaches, but an attempt to discover the island's soul — her people, her sea turtles, their nesting habits, the cause of the emerald waters, the origin of white beach sand, the underwater life of reef fish, wave dynamics, sunsets, moonrises and romance. The book also addresses the uniqueness of Marie-Galante, her sugarcane economy, the 19th Century wind mills (moulins) and her bloody and thrilling history.

This is one of the few places where a team of oxen pulling a wooden cart is a common sight, especially around the distilleries. Time has been kind to this small island, where life in the tropical sun moves at a more comfortable pace.

So please sit under a palm tree, sip a cold drink and read about the beautiful and exotic Marie-Galante. Let's get started.

What follows are a few practicalities you will need to know when visiting this island (traffic signs, English/French translations, etc.).

Language - Know These 4 Words

As an overseas Department of France the people of Marie-Galante speak French. While a few local people speak English, most do not. Thus, it is important to learn as much French as possible. Take an adult education course or take one of the many excellent free on-line courses. If you know only a few French words and have difficulty learning a new language, please learn these 4 words. "Bonjour" means hello or "good day" and "au revoir" means good bye. "Merci" means thank you. "S'il vous plaît" means please.

Four words, that's all. They are vital to communicating in Marie-Galante.

I hope you learn a few more words. You will need to know where the supermarket is and where the eggs are located. See the appendix for a listing of useful phrases.

Greeters

If you are not conversant in French you may want to hire a multi-lingual "greeter"' to be your friend on this special island, rent a car for you, show you the best place to buy groceries and answer your questions. Rates are reasonable.

Two "greeters" to consider are; Alison Rosinel, email: aylijah@gmail.com; phone: 590 690 36 6031 and 590 690 19 9329 and Stella and Richard Ardens, email: ardensrichard.gb@ hotmail.fr, Phone: 590 690 32 1800.

Telephones

Calling from Marie-Galante to another number in Marie-Galante is simple. All local calls begin with 0. If you dial to a land-line phone, the next 9 digit local number will begin with 590. If you dial to a cell phone, the next 9 digit number will begin with 690.

To call Marie-Galante from North America, dial 011 (the exit code), then 590 (the Guadeloupe country entry code) plus the 9 digit local number. The local number will begin with 590 if you dial to a land line, thus 590 will be dialed twice. The local number will begin with 690 if you are dialing to a cell phone.

To dial North America from Marie-Galante dial 001 then the 10 digit number beginning with the area code.

If you would like to place a call to or from another country visit http://www.howtocallabroad.com/

If you plan to use a cell phone while on the island, check with your phone company before traveling to determine the rates, programs and options for international phone service.

Electricity

Voltage in Marie-Galante is 220 AC, 60 Hz. Appliances designed for 110 AC volts require a transformer. Don't expect your inn to have 110 AC outlets or voltage transformers.

The good news is that most electronic devices (e.g. laptops, cell phones and camera battery chargers) are dual voltage, meaning they will work on 110 volts (in the United States, for example) and on 220 volts (in Europe and Marie-Galante). They are designed to work with frequencies ranging from 50 Hertz to 60 Hertz. In fact, many electronic devices will be damaged or destroyed by voltage converters, since the device already contains a converter.

To find out whether your electronic device is dual voltage, you will need to read the tiny words written on the bottom of your device or charger. You may need a magnifying glass to read the small print. If your device is dual voltage, you will see something like "Input 100 – 240V, 50 – 60 Hz" and will not need a voltage converter.

The electrical outlets on Marie-Galante do not accept USA plugs so you will need to bring a standard two-prong French plug adapter such as a Europlug or a Schuko adaptor. They cost about $10. Go on line and query electrical plug adapter, type E/F suitable for France, and other European countries. Some have double ports which allow you to plug-in two electrical devices at once. Remember the adapter does not convert voltage.

Time Zone

Marie-Galante is in the Atlantic Time Zone (GMT-4). When the eastern United States is on Eastern Standard Time, the time on the island is one hour later.

The island does not change to Daylight Savings Time. When the eastern US switches to Eastern Daylight Time, the time in the island is the same. Local time is usually indicated in the 24-hour format (1:15 p.m. is 13:15 or 13h15).

. . . .

Marie-Galante is at a latitude of 15.89° N, or about 500 miles south of the Tropic Of Cancer and 1100 miles north of the Equator. At this latitude, the length of each day is relatively constant, varying throughout the year from 11 hours from November to February to 13 hours from May to mid-August.

Some time between 5:30 and 6:30 PM each day depending on the time of year the sun will set. Sometimes between 5:30 and 6:30 AM (depending on the time of year) the sun will rise. Like the emerald world where time has stopped, the cycle of each day is constant.

Does it rain on this special island? Yes it does. Each day for 15 minutes a warm, gentle rain falls and refreshes the day. Let the rain kiss you. You deserve it.

. . . .

Island Time

As with most of the Caribbean, there is something called "island time." Visitors participating "in the race" want stores to open exactly when posted, meals to be prepared and served with "McDonald promptness" and schedules to be maintained. "Can't waste time, can't waste time" as they say in the "Pajama Game."

But the local people have a different point of view. Time is different on Marie-Galante. Life — every moment of it — is enjoyed. It is lived simply, deliberately, happily, with a smile. It is unhurried, relaxed and calm. There is time for you - for friends and family - for living close to nature. Life is sweet, not a race to the end. The best way to deal with "island time" is to simply relax and enjoy life. After all what is the rush? You will get to the end all too soon.

Island time is yours for the taking. It is free in this emerald world where time has stopped. When you come to Marie-Galante remember, *time is the treasure of life.* Sit back - read a book - take a nap. There is no race today.

Currency

The local currency in Marie-Galante is the Euro. Obtain Euros from your local bank before departure. It may take a week or more, so do this well ahead of time. Rely on major credit cards for larger purchases, and cash for small purchases. Be sure to check with your credit card company to see if you'll be charged foreign currency conversion fees (transaction service cost) on credit card purchases. A conversion fee is over and above the exchange rate amount. Bank of America does not charge a conversion fee! Visa and MasterCard are generally accepted at most established businesses. A universal currency converter is available at oanda.com.

You'll need your ATM card (called ABMs or *distributors des billets*) to obtain Euros for smaller purchases. You must establish a 4 digit PIN from your bank prior to departure or your card will not be accepted by ATMs on the island. This too may take a few days, so plan ahead. Traveler's checks are best carried as an emergency backup.

Although there is little crime in Marie-Galante, visitors should not leave cash or valuable items unattended.

Highway Signs

We may not think much about traffic signs; that's because they are uniform throughout the country in which we live. We follow them instinctively. In the USA there is a *"Manual on Uniform Traffic Control Devices"* published by the US Department of Transportation. The manual identifies the nation-wide standards for all streets, highways, bikeways, and private roads open to public travel. If you are visiting Marie-Galante from the USA, you may be immediately faced with a strange new set of traffic control signs —- French signs.

To assist you with rules of the road and ensure that you have a safe visit to the island, familiarize yourself with the Marie-Galante road signs shown in the Appendix.

Gas stations are not plentiful on the island, so make a mental note of your supply of fuel when you pass them.

. . . .

Don't expect "gasole" to be gasoline, it's not. It's diesel fuel.

. . . .

The three most common types of motor vehicle fuel *(carburant)* are:

- **SP95/E10:** Mixture of 95-octane gasoline/petrol (90%) with ethanol (10%).

- **E85** (Super Ethanol): A mixture of ethanol (70% to 85%) and gasoline/ petrol *(essence)* (15% to 30%, depending on the season). This fuel may not be suitable for most gasoline/petrol-powered cars.

- **Gasole** (Gasoil): Diesel fuel

If you plan to rent a car, your car will probably be a late model, and the type of fuel to be used should be specified somewhere on the car or rental agreement. (The fuel filler door or cap is a good place to look for a note on which fuel to use.)

There are rich sources of travel information in the following travel guides. I urge you to explore these resources.

Travel Guides

For information on flights, taxis, bus service, car rentals, hotels and entertainment visit one or more of the following travel guides.

French Caribbean - http://www.frenchcaribbean.com
Fodor's Travel Guide - http://www.fodors.com/
Trip Advisor - http://www.tripadvisor.com/
Lonely Planet - http://www.lonelyplanet.com/
Guadeloupe Travel Guide - http://www.guadeloupe-islands.com/
Marie-Galante Travel Guide - www.ot-mariegalante.com

To find a villa, inn or cottage, see the following.

www.lagalette.net/
www.iha.com/
www.homeaway.com
www.marie-galante-location.com

For a complete list of restaurants visit;

http://www.guadeloupe-islands.com

Geography of Marie-Galante (On-line)

In June 2006, IGN, the French agency responsible for producing and disseminating geographic information, opened Geoportail. Geoportail is a comprehensive web mapping service that provides on-line details of roads, contours, buildings, property parcels, marine hazards, hiking trails and more. To explore this web site go to; *www.Geoportail.gouv.fr.*

While Google Earth, the United States counterpart to *Geoportail,* provides a good aerial view of Marie-Galante, Google Earth does not provide the level of information and aerial resolution for Marie-Galante that is available from *Geoportail.*

If you enjoy hiking and island exploration, you will want more information than what is provided by the welcoming map found at the ferry dock. You will want to visit the internet for the on-line French equivalent of Google Earth.

Aerial photos showing land cover and physical features observable from the satellite are also available at www.cheminbleu.com.

Topographic Maps

In addition to tapping into the Geoportail on-line service, you will also want to obtain the French IGN Topographic Map, which is equivalent to the USGS topographic map. The IGN offers more than 2,000 topographic maps of France at a variety of scales as well as excellent maps of other parts of the world. All have an easy-to- use key in English, French and German and are beautifully produced.

By far the most popular maps are the IGN 1:25 000 topographic series. These maps are GPS compatible and meet the needs of walkers, horse-riders and campers. Maps are superbly detailed, a must for anyone wanting to explore Marie-Galante. They are simply the best walking maps you could ask for.

You can order the topographic map from Amazon com. Simply paste in the following Amazon book search request. *St-Francois / Marie-Galante / La Desirade (Guadeloupe) 2014: IGN4604 GT September 25, 2014.*

It can also be ordered from http://www.themapcentre.com

Locally, the map is available in downtown Grand Bourg at the Tourist Office and at Pegases Creation on Rue de la Marine (next to Footy's). A copy of the map will cost about $13. It is money well spent! Buy ahead of time. Place a copy of the map in your travel bag.

IGN is a French governmental administrative agency founded in 1940 to produce and maintain geographical information for France and its overseas departments and territories. Officially it is called the "Institut National de l'information Géographique et Forestière" (or National Institute of Geographic and Forestry Information). Earlier it was called the "Institut Géographique National" (or National Geographic Institute), thus the acronym IGN.

Open Street Maps

For an excellent street map for the island visit; openstreetmap.org.

"Openstreetmaps" is an organization of community map makers that contribute data on local roads, trails, cafés, railway stations, and much more, all over the world . This service and many other related services are formally operated by the Open Street Map Foundation (OSMF).

Grand-Bourg Beach

BEACH ETIQUETTE

"Manners are a sensitive awareness of the feelings of others. If you have that awareness, you have good manners, no matter what fork you use."

Emily Post

The French have a charming culture of etiquette. In fact the word "etiquette" is a French word. Islanders tend to have high standards for public behavior (manners) and appreciate visitors with those same values. It is considered polite to greet people with "bonjour" or "bonsoir" (if after Noon) on the beach and elsewhere for that matter.   If you ask an islander a question and fail to first say "bonjour," you will likely be greeted with a frown disapproving of your poor manners. If you follow the island's respectful decorum, the people of Marie-Galante will bend over backward to help you.

Marie-Galante's beaches are not crowded so it is easy to have good beach manners. There are few on the beach to offend. That said, you are a guest and should understand the customs and practices of civility on this island. Follow these few tips. They won't be posted.

PDA

Many French visitors publically display their affection (PDA) for their significant other. Whether you find it charming or uncomfortable, romance spills onto these island beaches. It is best to just ignore the PDA.

Beach Site

Locate your beach blanket and shade umbrella a minimum of 20 feet from the nearest sunbather. At 20 feet it is possible to listen to music quietly, have a private conversation and walk to and from the surf without traveling through the sites of others. Place your umbrella so that it doesn't block the view of neighbors.

Remember, your sandals and beach shoes kick up lots of sand particles so carry them until you are sure that you are on a hard surface or in the water. When shaking out a sandy towel and beach apparel, do so downwind from others.   If you are enjoying Frisbee, horse shoes or volleyball, find an area where the activity will not interfere with others.

Smoking

Cigarette smoke will carry some distance in the prevailing sea breeze. If you would like to smoke, it is good manners to retreat from the beach to a smoking area. It goes without saying that cigarette butts should likewise be extinguished and disposed of in a designated area; never on the beach.

Feeding The Seagulls

Feeding a seagull will attract more birds to the beach. Their waste is unsanitary. It is also difficult to enjoy a picnic snack with aggressive gulls begging for a handout. It is also unhealthy for the gulls. They begin to rely on bread and potato chips for their diet. Gulls need to forage for the plentiful fish and critters in the wash of the sea. When they come begging, resist the temptation to feed them. If you feed one, within 5 minutes you will have a flock of birds around you.

Dog Manners

Dogs are great companions however it is best to keep them off the beach. While we all like to think that our dog is well-mannered, it is important to remember that the canine social structure is quite different from ours. Inevitably their manners will conflict with ours.

Bark, romp, play, pee and poop that is the nature of a healthy dog. It is virtually impossible to contain their enthusiasm for life.

Dog waste is a health danger to humans. Even if dog waste is picked up, the U.S. Center for Disease Control and Prevention (CDC) reports that waste residue contains parasites including hookworm, ringworms, tapeworms, Salmonella and harmful bacteria that can cause kidney disorders and intestinal illness. The eggs from parasites can linger for years and present a pathway to humans through everyday activities such as walking barefoot.

Dogs are effective predators and often disturb shorebirds that are nesting. Dogs can crush or eat young chicks or flush the parents off nests allowing other predators easy access to them.

From late spring through early fall, sea turtles come to nest on Marie-Galante. To ensure survival of these endangered turtles it is vital that dogs do not disturb adult turtles, their nests, or hatchlings. Do not allow your dog to dig above the high tide line and do not bring your pets to the beach after dark when female turtles are laying eggs. Consider leaving your dog at home. You're on vacation.

. . . .

Pet travel regulations (PETs) govern travel of pets.
Airlines also have pet travel rules. Check with
your veterinarian and airline if you are considering pet
transport to Marie-Galante.

. . . .

Nudity

Nudity is not acceptable to local islanders. It is not liked at all! However, you will likely see topless women discreetly sunbathing on some beaches. Tourists walking about the beach topless are also occasionally observed. Full nudity is only appropriate in private coves and unpopulated remote beach retreats.

It's worth noting that for reasons ranging from skin cancer to creepy guys, French women are increasingly keeping their tops on. Accordingly, before shedding your bathing suit, look about you, be circumspect and discreet. It is also considered bad form to stroll off the beach and into town in your swimming suit. Use your fashionable cover-up whenever you leave the sand.

Young children (six years or less) can be totally naked on any beach and no one will mind. In fact, a child walking around in the saggy, waterlogged diaper might be the one who gets more disapproving looks.

Snapping a photo of attractive people in public without much (or any) clothing may be tempting for some, but don't. It is improper to take photos, stare or point.

Poisonous Manchineel Trees Are Marked
With A Red Band

The beaches of Marie-Galante are safe and enjoyable. Bring your chair, cooler and picnic basket and settle in for the day. Chances are you will find the perfect spot under the shade of a beautiful palm tree.

You are in a safe environment, that is, if you follow a few tips and use common sense. If you are worried about what is under the water, don't be. There are no giant squids lurking nearby to pull you to the dark deep, nor are there hungry sharks ready to snack on your toes. Shark and giant squid encounters make good movies but an attack on you is very unlikely. There were only 10 shark fatalities in 2014 -- world-wide. Residents do not recall there ever being a shark attack on the beaches of Marie-Galante. Put on your snorkel and mask and look at all the colorful fish and underwater marine life. Keep your distance and enjoy.

Rip Currents

Rip currents on the other hand are a real danger. They are responsible for 87% of beach drownings, so a basic knowledge of this peril and how to escape from a rip current is your best protection.

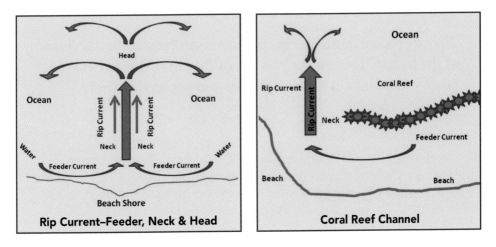

Rip Current–Feeder, Neck & Head

Coral Reef Channel

Longshore currents caused by large swells sweeping into the shoreline at an angle push water and transport sand down the length of the beach. When these currents meet a prominent rock outcropping, they may suddenly turn offshore in a fast, narrow current called a rip current. Rips are strongest and most dangerous on days with high surf.

Rip currents have three parts: the feeder current, the neck, and the head. While water from most waves simply returns to the sea the same way it came ashore (perpendicular to the beach), a feeder current is water returning from a wave *moving parallel to the beach* and along the landward edge of the beach. See diagram. This feeder current develops when the beach bottom has a depression or there is a break in the sand bar which provides the easiest path for the water to return back to the sea. This current moves quickly and with significant force, though it may not be obvious unless you are standing in it. A rip current can also occur when water moving parallel to the beach meets a rock outcropping or groin.

Water returns to the sea along a path called the neck. This neck is usually 30 feet (9 meters) or less in width. It is most dangerous because the water in the neck is channelized and flows rapidly away from shore. It can carry a swimmer out to sea at a rate of up to 6 miles per hour. Six miles per hour is faster than an Olympic swimmer can swim.

Within a single minute, a swimmer can be transported more than 500 feet out to sea. This experience can be extremely frightening to an unsuspecting swimmer, leading to panic, distress, exhaustion and ultimately failure of the swimmer to regain footing to the shore.

. . . .

Tip - If you encounter a rip current, swim parallel to the shore of the beach. This moves you out of the rip channel (neck). Once you swim out of the neck you can proceed to shore.

. . . .

Rip currents break down incoming waves. This flat water located between breaking waves, which appears to be safe water for your children, may actually be a rip current. It is a river flowing away from the beach out to the ocean stopping just beyond the breaking waves within the surf zone.

According to the United States Lifesaving Association (USLA), many drownings involve single swimmers. So "buddy up" and look after each other.

Know where the life rings are stored. If someone is caught in a rip current, throw the ring to the victim and pull him or her back to shore. If no life ring is available, remember that an ice chest or boogie board provides floatation which can keep the person afloat until rescue comes.

Manchineel Trees Are Poisonous

The manchineel (Le Mancenillier) tree grows along the coastline and beaches throughout the Caribbean, including Marie-Galante. *All parts of the manchineel tree are poisonous.* On Marie-Galante beaches the manchineel trees are marked with a red ring.

The French call the tree "arbre de mort" (tree of death). Ingestion of the apple-like fruit or for that matter ingestion of any other tree part can be lethal. Columbus who found a manchineel tree on Marie-Galante called the fruit "death apples."

. . . .

Don't seek shelter under a manchineel tree during a shower as the rainwater can carry the caustic and poisonous sap on to your skin. It is also inadvisable to have you picnic lunch under a manchineel tree.

. . . .

The tree can grow up to 50 feet in height. It is identifiable by the 1-2 inch diameter fruit which looks like a greenish yellow apple when ripe. It has shiny oval green alternating leaves 2 to 4 inches long with a very fine serrated edge. Each leaf has a small gland where the leaf joins the stem. The bark is reddish-to-grayish brown and deeply furrowed or cracked. Flowers are yellow green, but not conspicuous.

. . . .

Legend has it that Spanish conquistador Juan Ponce de Leon died from manchineel poisoning. Upon returning to Florida in 1521to lay claim to land and gold he was confronted by Indians. As you can guess the Indians weren't exactly going to hand over their land to him. In the struggle that took place, an arrow laced with manchineel sap struck Ponce de Leon's leg, leading to his long, drawn out death.

. . . .

The manchineel tree should not be confused with the maho tree which is similar in some regards. While both trees have yellow-veined green leaves, the maho tree has heart-shaped leaves, not oval. The maho has bell-shaped yellow flowers that turn to purple. Apples from the manchineel tree fall to the ground as yellow fruit. The ripe fruit of the maho fall to the ground as brown seed pods.

Manchineel trees produce a thick, milky sap that oozes out of the leaves, twigs, bark and fruit. The sap causes burn-like blisters when it comes in contact with the skin. It is advisable to avoid seeking shelter from the rain under a manchineel tree. The rain can rinse off the sap and burn your skin.

Medical Excellence

As an overseas department of France, islanders and visitors to Marie-Galante benefit from the same medical excellence as found in France. Good-quality hospitals, clinics and doctors are available on the island and in Guadeloupe. Not all doctors speak or understand English, so it helps to speak some French or at least have *Google Translate* handy. Here are a few medical centers.

The University Hospital in Guadeloupe *(Centre Hospitalier Universitaire (CHU) de Pointe-à-Pitre* Abymes, Tel: 0 590 89 10 10) is the major medical facility for the area. It has over 250 doctors on staff, 79 interns, and 900 beds. The services provided include cardiology, vascular surgery, orthopedic surgery, general and digestive surgery, pediatric surgery, urological surgery and most any other medical need you may call for.

The major hospital on Marie-Galante is Centre *Hospitalier Sainte-Marie, in Grand-Bourg* (Tel: 0 590 97 65 00). For emergency services while on the island call 112 the equivalent of 911in the US. This can be called from any mobile phone. For help from the fire brigade dial 18. For police assistance call 17.

OTHER SAFETY PRACTICES

1. **Bring Sun Screen.** The tropical sun is more intense than you think. You can burn in 20 minutes if unprotected.

2. **Swim With A Buddy.** Keep a close eye on children and your beach friends.

3. **Respect Rollers.** Large waves especially those breaking on shore may throw you into stones and rocks causing cuts, sprains and broken bones.

4. **Avoid Marine Life.** Coral and clam shells are very sharp; jellyfish tentacles, conch shells and sea urchin spines release venomous stings. Enjoy marine life from a distance.

5. **Wear Beach Shoes Or Sandals.** The sand can be very hot. Rocks hidden under the surf are sharp. Beach wear is vital!

6. **Seek Best Visibility.** For best visibility of underwater obstacles, experienced sailors recommend approaching the water depths with the sun over head or behind you, not in front of you.

TWELVE EMEALD BEACHES

What Makes Us Alive?

Scientists tell us we are 65% water, 18% carbon with hydrogen, nitrogen, calcium and phosphorous making up the rest. Stir in DNA, sugar, amino acids, lipids, a few lightning strikes and millions of years of evolution and somewhere along the way cells are formed and things come alive.

The Book of Genesis says from the dust of the earth God breathed life into Adam.

. . . .

Book of Genesis, Chapter 2.7
"...and God formed man from the dust of the earth and breathed into him the breath of life and man became a living soul."

. . . .

Whether you prefer the early explanation in "Genesis" or today's theory, there is no question that the world around us abounds with the God-given energy of life. It is not something you can see, touch or put in a bottle, but the difference between a living being and a corpse is obvious to all.

In Chinese and Japanese cultures this life force is called "Chi" (pronounced Chee). Chi is abundant in Marie-Galante - in her people, flowers, turtles, birds and beaches. These wonders increase our strength, refresh our soul and bring about a sense of inner peace. Being alive is exciting.

In the June 2010 Journal of Environmental Psychology research studies showed that being outdoors was the pathway to good health.

. . . .

"Studies show that being out-of-doors for as little as 20 minutes a day is enough to boost vitality, and this is over and above the heightened sense of well-being associated with outdoor exercise and being with friends. Nature is fuel for the soul. "

Richard Ryan,
Professor of Psychology, University of Rochester

. . . .

Visit Marie-Galante's beaches and breathe in the energy of life. Experience the paradise high. Become more alive. Increase Chi. See life as a child sees, enjoying it for the wonder and excitement that it is.

Mays Beach

Feuillere Beach

Marie-Galante's Beaches – *Best For:*

	BEACH	AMENITIES	BEST FOR:
1.	**Grand-Bourg Beach** (*Beach at Third Bridge*)	Bathrooms, Night Lighting, Shopping, Dive Rental/Instructions (nearby)	Beach Play (best of island), Twilight Swimming, Children, Beachcombing, Snorkeling, Sunsets, Family
2.	*Trail of Beaches*	None	Hiking, Picnicking, Bird Watching, (Solitude - best of island)
3.	**Petite Cove Beach** Plage de Petite Anse	Restaurants (nearby)	Parties, Picnicking, Swimming, Snorkeling, Walking, Sunbathing, Surfside Reading (best on island), Photography
4.	**Feuillere Beach** (Plage de la Feuillere)	Beach Bar/Snacks, Rentals, Fenced Playground, Bathrooms, Shopping, Restaurants, Groceries (nearby)	Kite Surfing and Water Sports (best of island), Sunrises, Moonrise, Sunbathing, Snorkeling, Swimming, Walking, Beachcombing, Photography (most scenic on island), Family
5.	**Taliseronde & Feuillard Beaches** (Anse Taliseronde & Anse Feuillard)	None	Moonrises (best of island), Sunrises, Snorkeling (best of island), Hiking, Picnicking, Surfing, Solitude, Reading, Sunbathing, Privacy, Beachcombing, Exploration, Turtle Watching, Star Spotting
6.	**Church Beach** (Anse de l'Eglise)	None	Romance (best of island), Picnicking, Sunbathing, Privacy, Reading, Solitude, Sunsets, Bliss

Marie-Galante's Beaches – *Best For:* (Continued)

BEACH	AMENITIES	BEST FOR:
7. **Old Fort Beach** (Plage du Vieux-Fort)	Bathrooms, Canoe Rentals	Sun Bathing, Swimming (adults), Hiking, Sunsets, Canoeing/ Paddle Boating, Ecology, Parties, Exploration, History, Snorkeling, Twilight Picnics, Family (best of island for diverse activities)
8. **Canoe Cove** (Plage de l'anse Canot)	Bathrooms	Swimming, Parties, Children, Hiking, Picnicking, Sunbathing, Twilight Picnics
9. **Mays Cove** (Anse de Mays)	None	History, Hiking, Swimming, Exploration, Sunbathing, Romance, Privacy, Solitude, Reading, Bliss, Photography, Surfing (best of island for beginners)
10. **Mosquito Beach** (Plage de Moustique)	None	Twilight Swimming (best of island), Picnicking, Sunbathing, Reading, Sunsets, Children
11. **St-Louis Beach** (Plage de St-Louis & Folle Anse)	Beachfront Restaurants, Groceries, Shopping (nearby)	Swimming, Picnicking, Walking, Turtle Watching, Sunsets (best of island)
12. **Three Islands Beach** (Plage des Trois Ilets)	None	Ecology (best of island), Walking, Swimming, Turtle Watching, Sunsets

Marie-Galante Beach Location Map

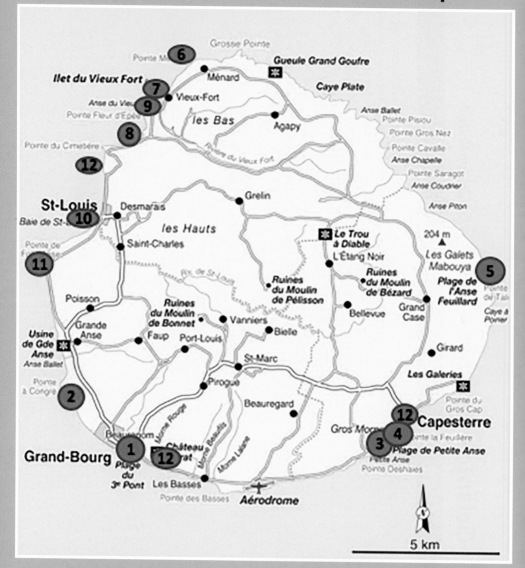

1. Grand-Bourg Beach
2. Trail of Beaches
3. Petite Cove
4. Feuillere Beach
5. Taliseronde & Feuillard Beaches
6. Church Beach
7. Old Fort Beach
8. Mays & Moustique Lagoons
9. Canoe Cove
10. St-Louis Beach & Folle Cove
11. Three Island
12. Beach Bars

Scale: 1 Inch Equals 1500 Feet

Grand-Bourg Beach

BEACHES OF GRAND-BOURG

Best of Island for Evening Beach Play

The shores of Grand-Bourg (pronounced as one word "Granbour") are sandy and delightful. They are protected from heavy waves by coral reefs about 1000 feet (300 meters) off shore.

How Do I Get There?

Traveling east on Route D 203 you will find several formal and informal beaches over a distance of 1.8 miles (3 kilometers). They unite the islanders with a place to socialize, watch the sunsets and pass the evening after a hard day's work.

Let's begin with the municipal beach, Grand-Bourg Beach or the "Beach of the Third Bridge" as it is sometimes called. It is located just as you depart downtown Grand-Bourg between the water and a strip of a dozen or so abandoned tin-sided homes that once housed the work force of the island. The beach is 780 feet (240 meters) long and about 200 feet (60 meters) wide. A small parking lot for 10 cars is accessible right off Route D 203 on the east end of the beach. The beach has picnic tables, bathrooms, showers and changing rooms. A dive shop where one can rent diving equipment or receive instructions is nearby.

Grand-Bourg children walk to the beach after dinner to enjoy the small soccer field right on the beach, the jungle gym or swimming under the lights. Adults enjoy watching the children play. They swim as a family. It is busy at sundown.

Remember it is OK for you to enjoy the beach just as the islanders do. Go barefoot. Sing. Smile at everyone. Laugh every chance you get. Hold hands.

The beach drops off into the water at a rate of 1 foot for every 10 feet of distance, which makes for a steady walk into deeper waters for swimming and wading. Non-swimmers and small children need to be watched carefully as in just 40 feet from shore they can be over their head. An area has been cordoned off for safe swimming. Here the bottom has been cleaned of spiny sea urchins.

The beach is not very busy during the day perhaps because it is exposed to the southerly sun or more likely because local residents are in school or working. There are 5 or 6 large coconut palm trees and 3 shelters that provide some shade.

If you are a people watcher, visit the beach at dusk after the sun's rays have subsided. It is a great place to sit, relax with a cold beverage and watch the children run and play. Many people come with their camera to catch the setting sun. The beach faces south so the sunset is on the west end of the beach. As with all sunsets on the emerald island, they are spectacular.

. . . .

You could call sea urchins the porcupines of the sea. Like a porcupine, sea urchins count on their long spines to deter hungry predators that may wish to eat them for a snack. In addition to the sharp quill that can be painful to touch, some sea urchin species have spines which will inject venom. The sting is reported to result in pain 3/4 of the intensity of a bee sting. It is best to stay clear of these cute creatures of the sea.

. . . .

For the beachcomber with a metal detector, chances are you will find something of value, as a small coin dropped on the ground can be quickly lost in the soft sand.

Pocket Beaches of Route D 203

As you depart from Grand-Bourg on Route D 203, the road follows along the southerly beach for a distance of several miles. The shore is close to the road in many areas. Along the way are several roadside restaurants.

Five small pocket beaches offer pleasant nooks to set up a chair and enjoy the rhythmic lapping of the waters. These nooks do not have formal names so let's call them (from west to east); Beaurenom Beach, Sunset Beach, Beach of the Babies, Loop Road Beach and Les Basses Beach.

Photo Credit Alisohn Rosinel

Sunset Beach

When the surf is up, these beaches are popular for kite surfing, especially along the pull-off on Route D 203 and at Les Basses Beach. Surfing can be frequently seen at sunset.

Beach at Beaurenom

At Beaurenom just 0.3 miles (500 meters) east of Grand-Bourg Beach there is a public parking area with room for 4 or 5 cars. The beach provides shade and public access to the velvet soft sand. Two picnic tables are available. A large piece of equipment perhaps used for pressing sugar from sugar cane lies in the water a few feet off the shore where it has been rusting for decades. Attention to maintenance and cleanup of trash would enhance the ambiance of this small pocket beach, although nothing can diminish the beautiful shoreline.

Sunset Beach

One kilometer further down D 203 before you reach the "Sun 7 Restaurant" is another narrow pocket beach. Access to the beach is down a short gravel grade. Sandals or beach shoes are needed if you have tender feet. Once on the beach you are again treated to soft white sand and overhanging vegetation, just perfect for snapping pictures of your vacation. This small beach has a big reward for those that like wading as you can wade hundreds of feet into the water before reaching water over your shoulders. Because you can touch bottom, it is a popular area for snorkeling and kite surfing.

The Sun 7 Restaurant is 800 feet (250 meters) east. Restaurant tables are right on the water's edge providing a relaxing place to spend some island time while waiting for dinner which starts at approximately 7 PM. Sit back, order a beverage and enjoy the beautiful sunset on the western horizon. The sunset casts its colors eastward right past your table. I am never disappointed with the splendor of these evening displays.

Beach of the Babies

About 0.3 miles (500 meters) past the Sun 7 Restaurant is the "Beach of the Babies" named by local residents because the eastern section of the beach is shallow (1 to 2 feet deep) just perfect for children to run and play. As with Sunset Beach, a prominent point has resulted in the deposition of beach sand in the bay allowing beachgoers to wade far out into the water. There are 2 pull-off areas on D 203 each suitable for a single car. Don't pull off too far as the end of the concrete apron has been undermined by wave action and you may get hung up. The beach has some shade, quiet blanket areas and is family friendly. Parking is limited to 1 space, which is perfect for sunbathers who don't like a crowd.

Several manchineel trees grow along the shore, not all of them are marked with the red band of paint. Be sure that children don't eat the small apple-like fruit and be careful not to seek shelter under a manchineel tree during a rain shower. If the tree sap mixes with the rain and drips on your skin it will cause a serious burn. All parts of the tree are highly poisonous.

Sunset at Sun 7 Café

The Path to Loop Road Beach

Loop Road Beach

About 150 feet further east down Route D 203 there is a right hand turn that takes you into a small residential neighborhood and then loops back on to Route D 203. Approximately 300 feet (100 meters) down this road there is a house on the right with a chain link fence covered with red Bougainvillea flowers.

Adjacent to the fence, a path leads a short distance to a beautiful beach about 700 feet long and 40 feet wide. The beach sand like most of Marie-Galante's beaches is mostly granulated coral. The east end of the beach is overgrown with sea grapes, while the west end of the beach terminates at a rocky end. A large manchineel tree grows here in the wooded buffer. There is a nice view of the island of Dominica which can be seen 32 miles off shore.

This is one of my favorite beaches. It is away from the traffic of D 203. As with most of Marie-Galante's paradise beaches, chances are you will have it all to yourself.

Loop Road Beach

Les Basse Beach

At the intersection of Beaufils Road and Route D 203 is Basses Beach. Parking is adjacent to the sidewalk and consists of a concrete pull-off with spaces for 10 cars end to end.

The small park has 3 picnic tables, trash cans and shade from a dozen palm trees, some of which are being undermined and eroded by waves breaking on to the beach. On the western end of the park are 4 large manchineel trees marked with the telltale red band of paint.

The waves are usually small making the beach safe for children to wade and play. The slope of the beach is gradual. Patches of turtle grass are just off shore and become heavier as you wade deeper into the water.

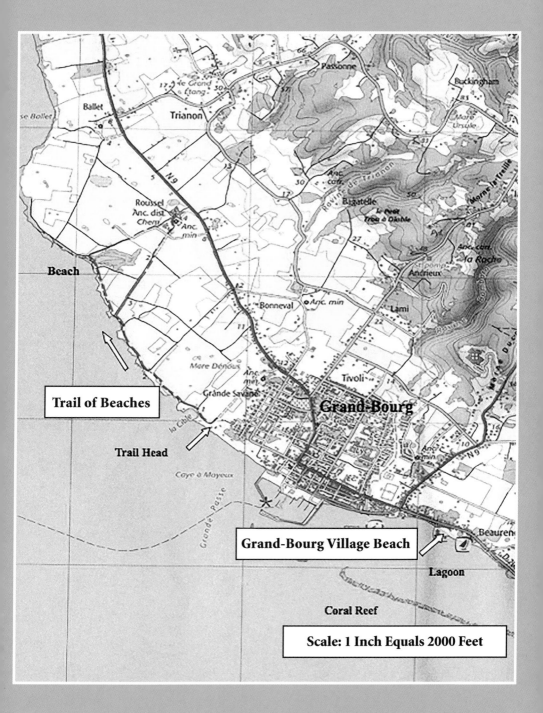

Trail of Beaches

Trail Head

Beach

Grand-Bourg

Grand-Bourg Village Beach

Lagoon

Coral Reef

Scale: 1 Inch Equals 2000 Feet

Mother and Baby on Beach of Grand-Bourg

·········· TRAIL OF BEACHES ··········

Best of Island for Solitude

For a 50 minute walk in intimate solitude along the shore of the Caribbean Sea follow the "Trail of Beaches." The trail takes you past a submerged beach with surging waves which have carved out small caves in the rocky coast and past a small beach of coral cobbles to an intimate sandy cove. The trail is lined with maho trees which protect the shore from erosion. In this walk with nature you will receive far more than you seek.

· · · · · · · · · · · · · · · · · · · ·

I go to my solitary walks as the homesick return to their homes.
Henry David Thoreau

· · · · · · · · · · · · · · · · · · · ·

Because the walk is level and open, it is well suited for families with young children. Don't forget to bring the picnic lunch.

Trail of Beaches

How Do I Get There?

Finding the trail head to start the walk is a little tricky. As you leave Grand-Bourg on Route 9N heading toward St-Louis there is a light duty industrial road on the left just past Vito's gas station. Look for the large sign for the El Rancho Restaurant/Movie Theater and turn left at the sign. Follow the road down the hill for approximately 500 meters to the area identified on the map as Grande Savane. There is a solid waste truck parking area on the left. Bear right down a farm road. Find a suitable place to park off the farm road and begin your hike.

You will be on a marked trail although the markers are old and need to be replaced. The trail follows the shoreline and leads to a lovely beach at a salt water pond about 1.25 miles (2 kilometers) from the point of beginning. It courses along a wagon trail through the back side of cane fields. Along the way don't be surprised to see cattle lounging on the trail. While they are staked out with a 30 or 40 foot chain, it is a little un-nerving to see a 1500 pound bull lying in the path in front of you. Be brave. Walk around the chained radius of the bull's grazing circle and pray that the bull is more interested in chewing his cud than that red beach towel you may have draped over your shoulder.

 The trail leaves the wagon road at times and meanders through the woods of "mother-in-laws tongues." Seaside maho trees are common along the way.

. . . .

Seaside maho trees (thespesia populnea) look very much like manchineel trees. A good way to tell them apart is to examine the leaves. The seaside maho has green heart-shaped leaves 4 to 5 inches in length with tapered tips while the manchineel leaves have an oval shape.

Maho trees grow to about 30 feet in height reaching a diameter of 8 to 12 inches. They tend however to grow with several trunks. Solitary hibiscus-like flowers bloom year-round and turn from yellow to red and purple before falling to the ground. The fruit is 1 to 2 inches in diameter. When ripe, the fruit is brown and leathery. The fruit is buoyant enabling the seed to be carried in the current of the sea to distant shores. The maho is salt-tolerant and can form a dense impenetrable stand to protect the shore from erosion.

. . . .

On the Path to the Beach

The trail will lead to a quiet sandy beach that provides a land bridge between a pond and the sea. The sand is fine coral, soft and inviting. The beach is crescent-shaped, about 600 feet long and 40 feet wide.

Rain Shelter

On the northern end of the beach is a well-built but vacant rain shelter that was constructed as a covered concession stand. It is hard to imagine that the stand was for commercial purposes as the beach and shelter are only accessible by jeep and farm tractors. Except for the lack of facilities of any kind, the concession stand seems perfect for a private party. While the beach is on a designated trail, it is unlikely that you will find any other people on the trail most days.

The trail loops out to the abandoned Roussel Chemical ruins and returns to a point just south of the salt pond, where the trail can be followed to the point of beginning.

. . . .

Mother-in-laws tongue (sansevieria trifasciata) also called snake plant is a green ground plant with a cluster of sword-shaped leaves growing in shaded dry soil. The leaves have light green or yellow bands that give the spikes the appearance of a snake. A study by NASA found that as a houseplant the leaves improve indoor air quality by absorbing toxins that may accumulate in the home environment.

. . . .

49

PETITE COVE BEACH

Surfside Reading (Best of Island)

Petite Cove Beach is "Plage de Petite Anse" in French. Plage means beach, petite means small and anse means cove in the English language.

Marie-Galante earns her West Indies reputation for beauty because of beaches like Petite Cove Beach located just a 10 minute drive from Grand-Bourg along Route D 203. If you are looking for a beach that has it all, white powdery sand and elegant coconut palm trees, you will want to enjoy this road-side jewel. With the warm tropical breeze, sea grape bushes which have been pruned into shade canopies, it is just the right place to read a book. It is also popular with islanders for Sunday family gatherings.

How Do I Get There?

As you travel north on D 203 you will hear the roar of the Atlantic as large waves roll in right up to the edge of the road. Stop and experience the thunderous power of the crashing waves. Petite Cove Beach is a short distance ahead.

Petite Cove Beach
(Plage de Petite Anse)

Hidden Beach

This beach has two parts, a hidden out-of-the-way patch of sand about 175 feet (50 meters) in length and the main beach. The hidden beach is nestled in a grove of manchineel trees, a few of which are over a foot in diameter. There is a pull-off for 2 cars just before you get to the main manicured beach of Petite Cove. You can only see this beach at the pull-off area. Most people don't know it is there. Moreover, their attention is directed to the swaying palm trees and beauty of the main beach just ahead. There is a short walk to a lovely sunbathing area protected on each end by coral ledges. This is separated by a short rock scramble to the main beach just to the north.

Main Beach

This main beach is about 1500 feet (450 meters) long and has a broad section where you will find several benches located in the shade of a large grove of coconut palms, 2 bath houses, trash cans and 2 parking areas, one allowing parking for 3 or 4 cars and the second providing parking for 10 cars or more.

Although the beaches are located on the Atlantic side of the island where swells are typically 4 feet (1.2 meters) in height, it has an off-shore coral reef (Caye au Vent or Cay of the Wind) which buffers the incoming waves, protecting swimmers and wading children. Make no mistake, the constant roar of ocean waves breaking over the reefs is a reminder of the incoming waves. You are at a mighty beach with swells that still find their way to shore. These can be a force to contend with for small children on a windy day.

Immediately in the breaking surf there is a 2 foot drop-off. Thereafter, the beach grade is moderate with a drop of 1 foot for every 20 feet of distance. The sand is soft, but there is an occasional toe-stubber so wear beach shoes. With the reefs and tamed surf, it is an excellent site for snorkeling and viewing a variety of tropical fish.

· ·

Are sea grapes edible?

Yes. Both animals and humans eat sea grapes. They are tasty when they turn a ripe, dark burgundy color. They are also used to make jam.

· ·

Petite Cove Beach

Walk To Capesterre

For those restless explorers who want to see what is around the corner, the adjacent Feuillere Beach (Plage de la Feuillere) is just a 10 minute walk north on Route D 203. Along the way you will pass three restaurants, LaPlaya, Touloulou and Anacardier. When you reach the north end of Feuillere a beach bar and a refreshing drink await you. A visit to the local tavern in Capesterre is another 5 minute walk on quaint village streets.

Le Touloulou is a Creole restaurant with tasty seafood located right on the beach. It is popular with people who enjoy the atmosphere of music from the bar with the harmonization of the lapping waves.

· · · · · · · · · · · · · · · · · · · ·

In French Guyana the "Touloulou" is the queen of the carnival who marches in the street on celebrations. She is a lady dressed elegantly from head to toe. She wears a colorful skirt, a flamboyant hat and long gloves. To avoid being recognized she may put on colored glasses, a wig, disguise her voice and wear a half mask in velvet or satin black , sometimes embellished with lace.

On Marie-Galante a Touloulou is simply a crab.

· · · · · · · · · · · · · · · · · · · ·

Le Touloulou has inside and outside dining and a beach disco adjacent to the restaurant that is busy Friday and Saturday nights. LaPlaya located across the street from Feuillere Beach is also a popular night spot. Here restaurant personnel speak both French and English. When you go past these restaurants inquire about their entertainment schedule and plan on returning for an evening of fun. Although you may buy a drink at any time, meals are not usually served until after 7:00 PM.

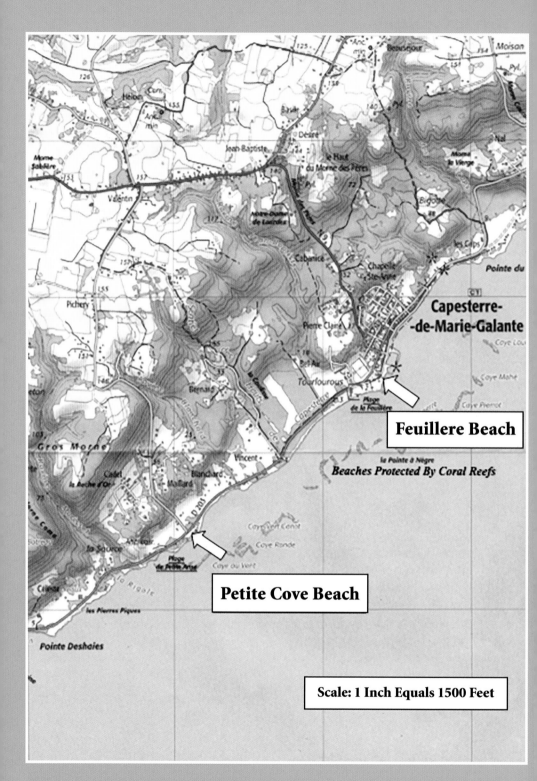

Feuillere Beach

Capesterre-
-de-Marie-Galante

Beaches Protected By Coral Reefs

Petite Cove Beach

Scale: 1 Inch Equals 1500 Feet

Feuillere Beach

FEUILLERE BEACH
(Plage de la Feuillere)

Best of Island for Kite-Surfing

Whether seen from underneath an expansive grove of swaying palm trees or from high above through the eyes of the angels, the view of the sun rising over the horizon on Feuillere Beach is stunning. Light reflects beautifully off the emerald lagoon. Shadows of 100 coconut palm trees are strewn over the white powdery sand. At sunrise or for that matter any time of day, it is one of the most beautiful beaches in the Caribbean, truly an unbelievable beach of delight. No wonder Feuillere Beach is one of the most photographed beaches in the West Indies.

The beauty and the lapping waves will overwhelm you with a sense of peace. They invite you to spread out a blanket and read a book, watch the children build sandcastles, take a swim in the warm waters or just sit back and take a nap - yes, take a nap! Don't feel guilty, you deserve it.

It is paradise in paradise; a magical place to etch new memories with special people in your life, memories to cherish when the time comes that you must part.

Kite Surfing on Feuillere Beach

Beaches are for Romance

. . . .

Windsurfing is a fun and exciting way to bring the whole family together. Age or sex is not an obstacle. Anybody can do it as long as they can swim and have no fear of water.

<u>You</u> can do it! Some people think that windsurfing is really hard. No way! The truth is … a good instructor using specialized training gear will have you gliding across the water in no time.

USwindsurfing.org

. . . .

How Do I Get There?

Located at the south end of the quaint hamlet of Capesterre on Route D 203, Feuillere Beach is over 0.5 miles (900 m) long and over 200 feet (70 m) wide. It is seldom crowded.

Activities

Feuillere offers something for everyone. A sports center where you can rent beach toys and windsurfing kites (and receive instructions) is sometimes open. Call ahead for reservations, – 0 690 71 28 78. *Le Sarha* beach restaurant is located on the south end of the beach and *Dantana Cafe'* and Le *Reflet de I'lle (Reflecting the Island)* beach restaurants are located on the north.

A reef, Caye a Tonnerre (Cay of Thunder), located 1,000 feet (300 meters) off shore, breaks up the high seas of the Atlantic, transforming the large waves into smaller spilling waves that release their last bit of energy as they come ashore. Swim with a buddy and watch children carefully as they can easily be swept off their feet.

If you want a beach with an active surf and no amenities, explore the southern end of Feuillere Beach where you will find sandy nooks mixed with rock outcroppings. You will have the beach all to yourself. It is rather open so bring an umbrella if you want shade.

Walking north toward Capesterre, the beach opens up and begins to display its beauty. Dozens and dozens of coconut palm trees and sea grapes come into view inviting you to rest in the shade, listen to the song birds and pass the time away. The sea grapes have been carefully groomed into canopies to shade your beach nest of blankets, cooler, book and radio. Snorkeling is excellent especially in deeper waters near the reefs. Deep silky-soft sand extends for 100 feet or more into the surf so you won't need your beach shoes. Go barefoot. Splash in the water as it flows onto the beach.

On the northern end of the beach you will find a fenced-in playground for children, benches, a boardwalk into town and the rental center. Parking is available for 10 or 15 vehicles. Three pavilions with picnic tables have been constructed. Across the street is an upscale hotel (Cap Reva) and there is also a local sports stadium.

**Feuillere
Boardwalk to Capesterre**

A boardwalk leads you to the hamlet of Capesterre where there are a number of small shops, a pharmacy, a supermarket, boutiques and several open air pubs and snack bars. Most take credit cards.

At the northern end of the beach, groins consisting of rocks almost the size of Volkswagens jut 200 feet out into the sea, the effect of which is to trap sand, nourish the beach and protect it from coastal erosion.

• • • • • • • • • • •

Capeserre is an old French seafaring term designating the side of the islands which first meets the trade winds, ie. the eastern side of the islands.

• • • • • • • • • • •

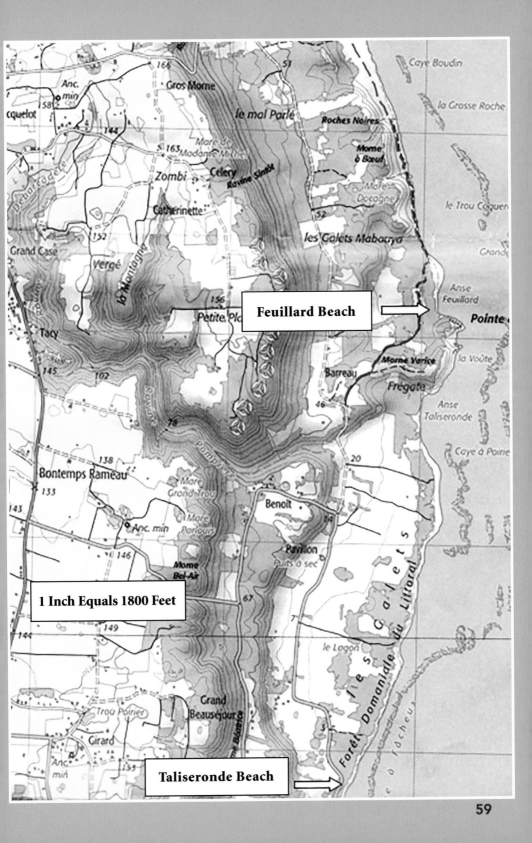

Feuillard Beach

Taliseronde Beach

1 Inch Equals 1800 Feet

59

Caliseronde and Feuillard Beaches

TALISERONDE AND FEUILLARD BEACHES

Best of Island for Snorkeling and Moonrise

Discover the wild and desolate Taliseronde and Feuillard coastal beaches. They are untamed, wind-swept and totally different than the other beaches of Marie-Galante. Neither beach has facilities, so plan accordingly.

How Do I Get There?

To find **Taliseronde Beach**, drive to the Village of Capesterre and follow the country road along the coast north 1.6 miles (2.6 kilometers). The road will turn away from the coast and up a hill but will again turn easterly and back to the coast. Here the road is lined with sea grapes providing a buffer between the road and the beach. Two pull-off areas offer a place to park. The beach is a short safe walk just beyond the sea grapes which makes for easy access to see the moonrise once a month or to watch a million stars light up the night. There is no light pollution on this span of the Atlantic Ocean. The nearest human settlement is thousands of miles away, in Africa.

Between May and October you will likely find sea turtle nesting sites in the sand. Look for the trademark wallow and "turtle walk" of turtles that returned to the sea from their evening of laying eggs.

Taliseronde Beach

Taliseronde is long and lonely being 1.2 miles (2 kilometers) long and 60 feet (20 meters) wide. If you rise with the sun, you can see spectacular sunrises on the sea's horizon, such as the "Orange Dawn" shown at the beginning of this chapter.

Take a walk on Taliseronde. Listen to the roar of the waves breaking over the reefs. It is a beautiful experience. There are places on this deserted beach where the sand ends, but returns again as you walk northward along the shore.

Feuillard Beach, which is similar in character to Taliseronde, is another 1.2 miles (2 kilometers) further north along the country road. When the road turns left, stay right and continue several hundred yards along a gravel road. Look for a gravel parking area on the right. Walk 0.4 miles (700 meters) down the hill on a shaded washed-out trail to an overgrown pasture. Continue through the pasture another 100 yards to the beach.

Feuillard Beach is 100 feet (30 meters) wide and 0.25 miles (400 meters) long. It is on the hiking trail to Anse Piton so you may meet an occasional hiking party. Otherwise, you will have the beach to yourself. Each end of the beach is rocky but the middle has deep sand. If you want to escape the hot sun a few paths lead back into the woods where a beach site can be set up.

. . . .

The lagoon off Feuillard Beach is colorfully named "Cockroach Hole," but no cockroaches are present.

. . . .

Hiking, Swimming, Snorkeling and Flying a Kite

A few shrubs and sea grapes provide shade and a place where you can spread a blanket. However, most of the shore is in the sun so bring drinking water and an umbrella. Both beaches are remote and great places to fly a kite, hike to the far reaches or just relax and watch the surf. Swimming is delightful in the protected lagoons behind the reefs but powerful currents exist in the unprotected waters. Portions of the beach are rock. Your mobile phone won't work in these locations so be careful to avoid an emergency.

Snorkeling is excellent, the best on the island, but be watchful of the currents, waves and reefs. Swim with a partner and begin your snorkeling near shore where you can match your skills with the challenges before you.

The Wild Woman of Feuillard

For years there were whispers among islanders of a ghost woman who lived in the wilds of Feuillard. In 2010, the "ghost of the woods," Clemence Noel, appeared after 40 years of living on wild chickens, eggs, fruit, fish and vegetables found in the local gardens. She lived by her wits and resourcefulness, sleeping in a hammock in the trees much like the native islanders before Columbus.

Jean Michel Dufour's chance meeting with the woman of the wild is described below.

. . . .

A few years ago a woman was found living in the wilds of Plage de Feuillard. She had been living in the thickets, eating leftovers from neighboring houses and provisions by those (few) who knew of her existence.

I met this woman in 2012 at the bend of a lost path while on a walk by the sea between Anse Strip and the path of Boreas. Her bare skin was wrinkled and leathery as old leather, as if she had faced the winds of the sea, the ocean spray and the bite of the sun.

She was almost naked, except for an old garbage bag over her head. She survived by scavenging small objects and towels left behind by carefree tourists.

Notes from Jean Michel Dufour

. . . .

Beachcombing

After a storm, the beaches are awash with Sargassum grass and all sorts of man-made items that have been discarded at sea or washed overboard. Beachcombers who enjoy searching for the unusual never know what treasures they will find for their collection or for their next sand castle or beach shrine. The discovery of an arrowhead or spanish coin will addict you to a lifetime of exploration and beachcombing.

Give way to your sense of whimsey and enjoy the "Robinson Crusoe" shelters on these beaches. These beach nests made from driftwood by ambitious beachcombers, provide primitive comfort and shade from the sun. The shelters are decorated with items discovered on the beach - fishing nets, heart-shaped coral, brain coral in the form of a skull, driftwood from far away places, sea fans, and all sorts of unexpected beach wash. All these add to the eclectic experience of spending an afternoon reading a book in one of the shelters.

· ·

Surfer Note

Sea water temperatures on Marie-Galante peak in the range 28 to 30°C (82 to 86°F) on the 2nd of September and reach their coldest on about the 15th of February, in the range 26 to 27°C (79 to 81°F). This year-round warm sea water mean that a rash vest and board shorts should be fine for surfing in any season.

· ·

Surfing

As with other beaches on the east shore, trade winds buffet the reefs with waves 2 to 4 feet high. Fortunately a chain of reefs dissipate the energy and reduce the size of the waves reaching the shore.

To the delight of surfers, Talliseronde and Feuillard are good surfing beaches. Coral reefs off-shore provide a surf break. When conditions are just right, the surf break will cause one side of the wave to break before the other. The wave is said to "peel" and may morph into a barrel wave.

When a wave "peels," surfers enjoy riding back and forth across the crest as it slowly breaks, or they may streak through a wave barrel in hopes of a classic Kodak moment. Listen carefully to the music of the waves. Sing. You may be joined with the faint five-part harmony, *Catch A Wave! Catch A Wave!* Are those the Beach Boys you hear above the roar?

. . . .

"A beach is not only a sweep of sand, but shells of sea creatures, the sea glass, the seaweed, the incongruous objects washed up by the ocean."

Henry Grunwald

. . . .

. . . .

"When you arise with the dawning sun,
think of what a precious privilege it is to be alive –
to breathe, to think, to enjoy, to love."

Marcus Aurelius

. . . .

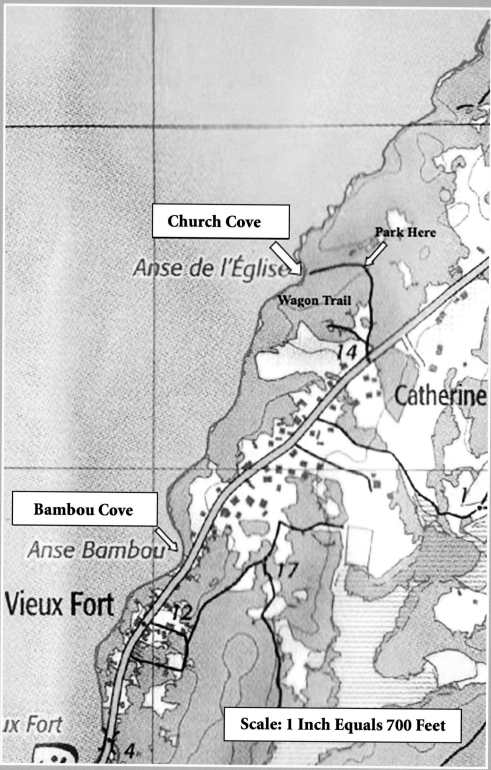

Church Cove

Park Here

Anse de l'Église

Wagon Trail

14

Catherine

Bambou Cove

Anse Bambou

17

Vieux Fort

12

ux Fort

4

Scale: 1 Inch Equals 700 Feet

CHURCH COVE
(Anse de l'Eglise)

Best of Island for Romance

Gradually, if I go with courage and wisdom, I arrive at my destination, a place called paradise. It is not a land free of struggle, a realm devoid of pain or grief. But it is the place where I feel at home, where I am supposed to be.

Richard Bode, from "Beachcombing at Miramar"

If you are looking for a secluded hideaway that is off the beaten track, you will enjoy Anse de l'Eglise or "Church Cove."   Like the island itself, Church Cove is a beach forgotten, tucked away where no one can find it; at the end of a series of beaches that extend from Saint Louis to Old Fort Beach. It is with some hesitation that I reveal its location because some readers will want to visit it, thus defeating the very intimacy and solitude that makes it special.

Church Cove
(Anse de l'Eglise)

How Do I Get There?

The beach is about 0.36 miles (580 meters) north of Old Fort Beach. Look for a wagon road on the left as you travel north. The road is just as you leave the residential area of Catherine. Follow it, bearing right at the first fork until you arrive at a turn-around about 330 feet (100 meters) from the main road. Park here as the path to the beach is unsuitable for motorized vehicles. The rocky path is about 500 feet (150 meters) long down a medium grade to the beach. The small island Vieux-Fort Islets nesting home of the sooty tern, can be seen in the distance off the shore to the south.

· ·

The sooty tern is a common sea bird in the Caribbean. It can be identified by its almost black back and wings with the dark brown crown and white patches on the forehead and breast. They call "ker-wacky-wack."

A major problem is the large-scale collection of eggs which are referred to as "booby eggs."They are considered an aph-rodisiac by local hunters.

· ·

There are no amenities except for the natural beauty of pure white coral sand and the shade from the trees above the high water swash zone. The beach is buttressed at each end with rocks. Fallen rocks are present in the wading area so be careful swimming when the surf is up.

Romance

As beaches go, it is small, only 115 feet (35 meters) long, just perfect for lovers who want to enjoy a picnic and be alone. Rocks in the water and waves mean that you probably won't be skinny dipping after dark.

Go to Church Cove for sundown and see the lovely sunset over the island of Vieux Fort off the southern end of the beach.

Bambou Cove

This small beach is located between Old Fort Beach and Church Cove right on the edge of the road. Parking is limited. The soft silky beach is a good place to launch a small boat. It is protected from the wind. Many use the beach to test snorkeling equipment, watch the small fish swimming among the rocks on the north shore or to take a quick swim to cool off from the hot mid-day sun.

Sunset at Church Cove

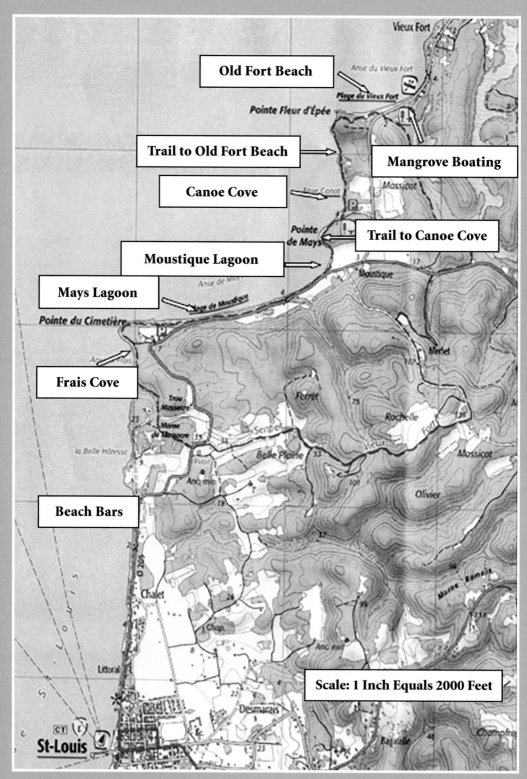

Old Fort Beach

Trail to Old Fort Beach

Mangrove Boating

Canoe Cove

Trail to Canoe Cove

Moustique Lagoon

Mays Lagoon

Frais Cove

Beach Bars

Scale: 1 Inch Equals 2000 Feet

Old Fort Beach
(Plage du Vieux Fort)

OLD FORT BEACH
(Plage du Vieux Fort)

Best of Island for Families

Of all of Marie-Galante's beaches Old Fort Beach is a delight for active families who like hiking, kayaking, swimming and snorkeling. Set up the volley ball net on the beach if you wish. There is plenty of room. Blend in a lavish picnic BBQ at one of the sheltered picnic tables and you have a day's outing sure to tire the whole family. Because there are lengthy hiking and kayaking excursions and trails to the nearby beaches of Canoe Cove and Moustique Beach, bring walkie-talkies so you can keep in touch with adventurous and straying members of your party.

The beach forms a crescent that extends as far as the eye can see being nearly 0.4 miles (620 meters) long and 50 feet (15 meters) wide. On the southwest end there is a private sandy lagoon nestled behind some rocks where you can sunbathe, swim, take a nap and listen to the lapping waves. It is a private place where you can get rid of tan lines while maintaining a modicum of modesty. Innocent nudity on Marie-Galante's beaches is accepted as it has been since the Garden of Eden when time began.

How Do I Get There?

From downtown St-Louis take Route D 205 north about 1.8 miles (3 kilometers) to the hamlet of Moustique. As with the seductions of the sirens, you may never reach Old Fort Beach because you will pass the beautiful beaches of May's Cove (Anse de Mays) and Moustique (Mosquito) Beach. Both have beautiful emerald lagoons that will tempt and seduce you to their shores.

Come this way, honored Odysseus and listen to our singing;
for no one has ever sailed past this place until he has listened to
the honey-sweet voice from our lips.

From The Odyssey

At the Moustique hamlet, take a left on an asphalt secondary road at the guide-board to the Old Fort Beach. It is located just 0.6 of a mile (1 kilometer) further north.

View

Prominently viewed from the beach is the island of Vieux Fort (I'let du Vieux Fort) located about 0.6 miles (800 meters) off shore. The faint silhouette of four palm trees can be seen on the center of the island.

Facilities

Six shelters are scattered among the palm trees over the length of the beach. Most of the shelters are equipped with a picnic table, BBQ grill and trash cans. The road runs along the shore where there is ready access to the shelters. If you are out for an evening drive, Old Fort Beach is a perfect place to stop, sit down at a picnic table with a snack and watch nightfall.

A unisex bathroom is available at the kayak rental kiosk. Along the road, the Office of National Forests has cordoned off demonstration plots where visitors can see native seedling trees and natural beach grasses growing.

Snorkeling

Old Fort Beach is noted for good snorkeling in the deeper water where coral is found. Just beneath the twinkling, satin surface of calm waters swim fish of a hundred different shapes and colors. Bring your reef fish identification book to enhance your enjoyment.

Hiking

A popular itinerary is to set up a picnic site on the beach and plan a hike to explore the area. The two most popular hikes are; 1) the hike from Old Fort Beach to Canoe Beach; and 2) the hike into the mangroves of La Riviere du Vieux Fort (Old Fort River) to the observation deck and back.

Hike #1 - Point Flower Sword Trail (Old Fort Beach to Canoe Beach) -

From the parking area at the south entry to Old Fort Beach, pick up the trail marked with a

Mangroves
La Riviere du Vieux Fort
(Old Fort River)

green stripe on the trees and rocks. Wear good footwear as there are some nasty sandspurs in the grass near the parking area.

At first, the trail is very steep but after a short hand-over-hand scramble the trail mellows out, up over the limestone bluff of Point Flower Sword (Pointe du Fleur d'Eppe), through a shaded woods overlooking the emerald waters, and then down the bluff to the popular beach of Canoe Cove (Anse Canot). It is a pleasant 25 minute walk. At this point you can enjoy Canoe Beach for a while and plan your return, either along the service road or back along the Point Flower Sword Trail. Extending the hike over Pointe de Mays to Moustique Beach is also an option that provides a great view of the vast ocean and the island of Guadeloupe.

Hike #2 - Old Fort Mangrove Trail

This hike begins on a boardwalk on the east side of the road along Old Fort Beach, next to the mangroves of La Riviere du Vieux Fort (Old Fort River). At the end of the 100 foot boardwalk the trail breaks into a damp woodland road for a distance of 0.4 miles (650 meters).

Here the trail meets a boardwalk leading to a bird observatory overlooking a long serpentine section of Old Fort River. The river at this point is 200 feet (60 meters) wide, looking more like a small lake than a river. The observatory has a roof to offer shelter should you encounter a short rain shower.

While the trail is shaded and flat, it is otherwise plain and out of sight of the river and mangroves until you reach the observatory. A more scenic alternative is to rent a kayak or paddle boat (available on site) at the beachside kiosk and paddle up to the observatory. Keep your eye open for small turtles which inhabit the mangrove. This water route takes about 1 hour round trip. Call ahead, 0 590 97 13 72 to be sure the rental kiosk is open.

Surfing/Swimming

While the sandy shore implies that the sand extends into the water, beware! Most of the beach has some ledge rock and toe stubbers hidden in the surf. Given that the waves break close to shore, surfing and swimming is dangerous at many locations, especially for children. If you decide to surf or swim, choose your location carefully.

History

When you walk the shores of Old Fort Beach you can't help but wonder who has walked there before you. Was there a native village at this site? What was life like? Who else may have come ashore? Were there pirates, priests, explorers, settlers? Were they there in peace or conflict?

Not much is left of the Old Fort, not even its history. We do know that the fort was built in 1648 by French colonists for protection from warring Caribs. It is the first European settlement on the island and the site of conflicts and fierce skirmishes between the Caribs and new settlers. The beach is sometimes called Plage du Massacre in memory of those who were massacred by revengeful Caribs in 1653.

For more on the history of Old Fort and Marie-Galante you may wish to read, *Chronological History of the West Indies: In Three Volumes, Volume 3* By Thomas Southey.

. . . .

Cenchrus (sandspur, sandbur, buffelgrass) is a family of grasses widespread on the Caribbean islands. It is a perennial grass 6 to 30 inches tall that grows in sand and require little water to thrive. The grass produces a burr consisting of eight to forty sharp, barbed spines that lodge in clothes, exposed feet, and fur. They can be painful to step on and tend to stick to your skin. To un-stick a burr, spit on your fingers to pull them out. Don't squeeze. Spit keeps the barb from clinging anew.

. . . .

Canoe Cove
(Anse Canot)

CANOE COVE
(Anse Canot)

(Best of Island for Parties)

Just north of Moustique Beach is Canoe Cove (Anse Canot), the third of four beautiful beaches in a row off Route D 205 north of St-Louis. Like Mays, Moustique and Old Fort beaches, Canoe Beach is not exposed to the trade winds, thus it is usually calm, ideal for swimming, sunbathing and safe for children. The well shaded beach is 600 feet (190 meters) long and 130 feet (40 meters) wide. Except for the south end of the beach which has large fallen rocks from the bluff at Point De Mays, children play on the beach with abandon, enjoying the sand which runs into the deep water of the cove.

In the shaded woods behind the beach are 5 shelters with picnic tables. Some have grills. At the parking lot there are toilets, but they are not always open for use.

How Do I Get There?

To find the beach, travel 2.5 miles (4 kilometers) north of St-Louis along Route D 205. Take a left at the hamlet of Moustique on to a local paved road. About 950 feet (290 meters) down the road there will be a sign to Canoe Beach. A parking lot with spaces for 20 or more cars has been constructed above the beach. The beach is about 300 feet (100 meters) beyond the parking lot down a slight slope on a narrow concrete sidewalk.

Activities

Discrete topless sunbathing by tourists is common on this beach as it is on many of the island beaches. The beach is also a popular party beach and a top choice among boaters who come to this emerald cove not only for its beauty and satin soft sand, but to get some exercise and escape the confines of their small quarters. As a bonus, the cove is protected from the winds by the surrounding cliffs.

Many beach-goers make Canoe Cove a base for a day-long outing. They bring their kayaks, backpack, picnic lunch, towel and snorkel and hike to neighboring beaches at Moustique Lagoon and Old Fort, enjoying each for a few hours over the course of the day.

On the south end of the beach is a short trail over Pointe de Mays to Moustique Beach. On the north is another short trail over the white cliffs of Pointe Fleur d'Eppe leading to Old Fort Beach. Each hike can be completed in about 25 minutes. Good footwear is needed.

Snorkeling is excellent. A variety of tropical fish can be found at the base of the rock bluffs off Pointe Fleur d'Eppe and Pointe De Mays located at each end of the beach.

Canoe Cove

Canoe Cove is a popular party beach.

. . . .

Saltwater Facts

- Minerals washed from the land for millions of years have created Earth's saltwater oceans, providing a perfect living environment for millions of life forms; fish, coral, reptiles, invertebrates and micro organisms of all kind. Far more species live in our oceans than on the land.

- The concentration of minerals (predominantly sodium and chloride) in seawater is about 3.5%. Stated in another way, there is about one half cup of salt for every gallon of water in the ocean. Because of the added minerals and the increased density, objects are more buoyant in saltwater than fresh water. Swimming is enjoyable at Marie-Galante's beaches because of the slightly greater buoyancy and ease in our saltwater seas.

. . . .

Mays Beach and Moustique Lagoon

MAYS BEACH
AND
MOUSTIQUE LAGOON

Mays: Best of Island for Surfing (Beginners)
Moustique: Best of Island for Sundown Swimming

How Do I Get There?

About 1.9 miles (3 kilometers) north of St-Louis on Route D 205 are the peaceful shores of Mays Beach and Moustique Lagoon. Together, these silky white beaches are nearly 1.0 mile long (1.6 kilometers). You can't miss the gravel parking area as you descend to Mays Beach from Trou Massacre Hill. It has spaces for 20 cars but seldom are there more than 6 or 7 in the lot. There are also several pull-off areas with room for 1 or 2 cars on the road as it passes the beach, so you can pull right up to your favorite spot.

· · · · · · · · · · · · · · · · · · ·

In French moustique means mosquito. Don't be concerned about mosquitoes. They lay their eggs in stagnant waters— ponds, marshes, swamps and wooded wetlands, not at beaches. Although you may encounter an occasional mosquito, you won't find the beaches of Marie-Galante infested with them.

· ·

Swimming

Except for the western end which has some sharp coral rocks, Mays Beach is an excellent family beach with sand that extends into deep water. It is a safe place to swim and kayak and to teach children the skills for enjoying water activities.

Romantic Sunsets

Sunsets on Mays Beach are, well – a"MAYS"ing! The western end of the beach at Pointe du Cimetiere looks out over the setting sun. It is perfect for sunsets! So when evening falls as will happen each day, walk along the coast to the west with your lover and find a private lagoon. High overhead, the setting sun will give way to a sea of a million stars that will wash the beach and incoming waves in stardust. Plan a twilight picnic with crackers, cheese and a bottle of the finest French wine.

Hiking

If you like hiking and always wonder what is around the corner, you will like Mays Beach. Walking westward along the waterfront path of white spider lilies and mother-in-laws tongue you will come to a marked trail that leads to a deep ravine and the sites of the Trou Massacre (Massacre Hole) and Morne du Massacre. Marked with green stripes, the trail ascends to the massacre site. The site has been dedicated to the memory of Old Fort settlers who were massacred by the Carib Indians in 1653.

. . . .

Trou Massacre (Massacre Hole): The first colonists chose to settle around the lake that now forms the estuary of the river called "Old Fort." It was also the place where fierce Carib warriors had long lived. In 1653 in retaliation for the rape and looting in Dominica by Martinique settlers, the natives massacred 50 innocent settlers of Marie-Galante, impaling their heads on poles for display on the beach. Historians report, "The flesh of the dead was likely eaten."

. . . .

If you choose to take the path less traveled along the shore instead of the marked trail to Massacre Hole, you will encounter one intimate lagoon after the other, each separated by rocks. The sandy mini-beaches in these lagoons will be just large enough for your beach blanket. Ledges and rocks extend into the water so be careful when you wade or swim.

Moustique Lagoon

Rounding the Pointe du Cimetiere (Point of the Graveyard) on a poorly traveled trail through the underbrush you come upon a 20 foot wide 200 foot long beach called Frais Lagoon. It is remote and private with a nice view of the setting sun. The beach is not wide so it will be flooded when a high tide and an active surf occur at the same time.

Surfing

Mays Beach is a good place for beginners to pick up the skills of surfing. While the beach often has calm waters, when the surf is up, the beach produces spilling waves- surfer waves. Beginners can launch close to the shore and ride the waves to the sandy beach. Waves are tame and the silky soft sand provides a safe landing. It is favored by families because children can body surf and boogie board to the delight of watchful and photographing parents.

Moustique Lagoon

The popular Moustique Lagoon is located at the northern end of Mays Beach. Waters here are always agreeable. Islanders know which beaches are best. They bring their children to Moustique because of the calm protected waters, sandy bottom and beautiful sunsets which occur each evening on the horizon off Pointe du Cimetiere. Twilight swimming is both safe and delightful.

A small parking area off Route D 205 has space for 5 or 6 cars. The beach is just feet away from the parking area making it convenient to bring your beach chair, umbrella, snorkel and all the other stuff that will make a day in the sun memorable.

There are no bathroom facilities or other amenities at Mays and Moustique beaches.

Twilight Swimming at Moustique Lagoon

Trail To Canoe Cove

Moustique Lagoon has an easy trail on the eastern end of the parking area that leads through the woods up over Pointe de Mays and down to Canoe Cove. It is shaded. The breeze at the top is refreshing in the warm tropical day.

. . . .

There is something magical about an evening swim on Moustique Beach;
when the blazing sun is setting at the end of the day, or a
full moon drapes the beach in exotic shadows or the stars magically
display a million twinkling lights. As Nora Roberts said;

"Magic exists.

Who can doubt it, when there are rainbows and wildflowers,
the music of the wind and the silence of the stars?"

Nora Roberts

. . . .

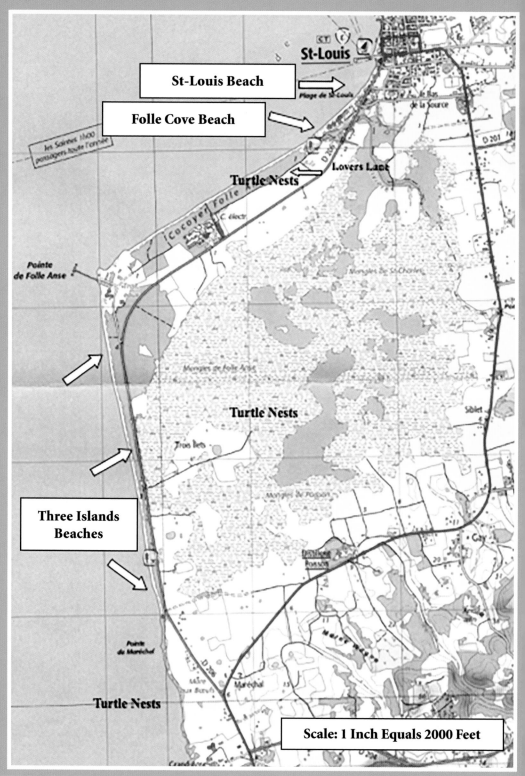

St-Louis Beach

Folle Cove Beach

Turtle Nests

Lovers Lane

Turtle Nests

Three Islands
Beaches

Turtle Nests

Scale: 1 Inch Equals 2000 Feet

St-Louis and Folle Cove Beaches

ST-LOUIS
AND
FOLLE COVE BEACHES

(Best of Island for Sunsets)

How Do I Get There?

St-Louis (pronounced senlwi) is 1 of 3 hamlets on the island. It is located on the west coast off Route D 206.

Two beaches are connected; the downtown beach and the St-Louis Beach Park (Folle Cove Beach) located 0.25 miles (400 meters) southwest of downtown on Route D 206. A concrete sidewalk connects Folle Cove to the downtown so a walk from the beach to downtown is safe and a good way to get some exercise. Why not take a mid-day stroll into town for a leisurely lunch?

Finding Folle Cove Beach can be a little tricky as it is marked only by a small sign that says "plage" along with a directional arrow for you to follow. Look for a dirt road off Route D 206 that leads to the palm trees on the beach a short distance away.

Facilities

The downtown beach is bordered by residences and small shops. Beach bars are located right on the sandy shores where beautiful sunsets can be seen from the tables every evening.

Local children use the beach for pick-up volleyball, soccer or for searching the beach for treasure, red crabs and other critters. For St-Louis residents, the beach is just another strip of sand, just another beach, and thus it has not been developed to its recreational potential. The beach is open to the public, just perfect for a morning stroll with a cup of coffee. If you have a metal detector, search for artifacts from sunken ships lost in antiquity.

Anchorage

St-Louis is one of the two anchorage sites for yachts on the island, the other being at Grand-Bourg. A large dock in the center of the town extends about 300 feet (100 meters) into deeper water to accommodate ferries traveling to and from Guadeloupe and for deeper draft boats. Water depth is 8 to 11 feet shelving to shallower depths as you approach the shore. The bay has spaces for 20 moorings north of the dock and a dozen or so south of the dock. The southern anchorage is the more pleasant of the two.

Boaters come ashore for beach time, exercise and shore services. Within walking distance of the beach is a post office and shops where you can rent cars, scooters, sailboards and Hobiecats.

Hiking

If you like hiking, it is possible to hike several miles south along the shore from St-Louis to a point near the sugar factory without departing from the soft sand of the beach.

Folle Cove Beach

Folle Cove Beach which is part of the greater St-Louis Beach is 320 feet wide at the park but extends southward narrowing to 50 to 100 feet for a considerable distance. The beach is ideal for a day of picnicking, swimming and hiking with the family. Camping, fires, picking flowers or disturbance of wildlife are not allowed.

St-Louis Looking North from Village Pier

Here you will find two shelters and six or seven picnic tables. You are able to pull your car right up to the shelter for tailgate picnics. On the north end of the beach are bathrooms. They are not always open. Lying derelict across a small creek is an interesting old rusted steel bridge that must have been used 100 years ago. The north end of the beach is interrupted with a petroleum storage terminal. A filling platform located about 300 feet off shore and an underwater pipeline are used to fill the tanks. Anchorage near the pipeline and filling platform is prohibited.

Boaters and beachgoers are treated to very calm waters and soft white sand which provides safe footing free of rocks and hazards. A swimming area about 150 feet (50 meters) in length has been cordoned off with floating ropes for water safety, but most people just wade in anywhere along the beach. The footing is sandy and swimming is delightful. The beach slopes about 1 foot in every 30 feet of distance. It is ideal for children.

The beach faces west providing a nice view of Guadeloupe and the emerald green water that blends seaward into the deep royal blue of the Guadeloupe Channel.

Sunsets

Sunsets are spectacular. The beach is perfectly positioned for an unforgettable sundown moment! Plan to arrive 20 minutes before sunset and stay 30 minutes after sunset to experience the full beauty of the sky afire as the sun dies on this paradise island. Look for the green flash that occurs just as the sun sinks below the horizon. Enjoy twilight. Watch as the sun gives way to a nighttime of blue, exotic shadows and starlight. Wonder about stars and the vastness of the universe. Will we ever know what wonders lie beyond our world?

From Folle Cove Beach southward, a narrow sandy beach runs continuously along the nature preserve for a distance of 1.25 miles (about 2 kilometers), past the power generating plant to Pointe de Folle Anse the island's major port for exporting sugar and rum products. If you like to hike and explore the water's edge, you will like this long stretch of beach. It is there for your environmental enjoyment.

In back of Folle Cove Beach is lover's lane, a wagon road that separates the sugar cane field from the park. If you are looking for an intimate place to sunbathe and be alone with someone special, follow the wagon road 600 feet or so to a pull-off. Park here (there is room for only 1 car) and walk through the woods a short distance to a private nook, perfect for a romantic sunset. The sand is soft and the waters are calm. Take a twilight swim. Keep your clothes dry. You won't need a bathing suit here.

South of Folle Cove Beach are important green turtle and hawksbill turtle nesting areas protected under the Coastal Protection Act and managed by the Office of National Forests of France. The protected area consists of coastal woods and 1.6 square miles (406.7 hectares) of wetland and diverse woodland located between Route D 206 and Route 9.

From late Spring to early Fall these turtles come ashore after dark to lay their eggs. If you are visiting the beach during the nesting season don't be surprised if you stumble on one or more of these endangered reptiles. Look for large hollows in the beach sand; telltale signs that a turtle may have a nest at that spot. This nesting site is important to the future population of these Caribbean turtles.

This special environmental area also provides habitat for a variety of birds and wildlife. If you are a bird watcher, bring your bird book and binoculars.

A few years ago, there was a large population of stray dogs and raccoons scavenging a nearby solid waste landfill. Their instinct is to dig for turtle eggs and eat them. It is important to keep all dogs away from the beach. The landfill has now been capped and fenced so stray dogs and raccoons are less of a problem. Today, the beach is most threatened by "dog's best friend" – man.

Folle Cove Beach Looking Southwest

Three Islands (Trois Ilets) Beach

THREE ISLANDS
(Trois Ilets)
BEACH

(Best of Island for Ecology)

Why are we drawn so irresistibly to the beach and the sea? What lies hidden within us that pulls us there? And when we get there, what is it that we find that draws us back and back again? Is it the sound of the waves, the warmth of the sun, the peace, the solitude or the sea of twinkling stars in the night?

To help answer these questions, visit Three Island Beach.

How Do I Get There?

The Three Island Beach (Trois Îlets) is a calm beach of fine white sand about 30 feet wide and 1.25 miles (2 kilometers) long located on Route D 206. This linear beach is south of the Port at Folle Anse.

There are seven pull-off areas along the road, each accommodating parking for 1 or 2 cars. Some pull-offs have picnic tables, some have rain shelters and others offer nothing but a path through the woods to the beach.

Activities

Because of the length of the beach, there is always a quiet place to find peace and privacy. The beach is just a short walk from Route D 206, so it is easy to tote a chair, cooler and book to the water's edge. Overhanging the beach are sea grapes and woods that provide shade from the tropical sun. Swimming is pleasant and safe. In clear weather, the beach offers a superb view of Marie-Galante's mother island, Guadeloupe. For the explorer, this beach provides an opportunity to stretch your legs, get some exercise, find a few sea shells and discover beach treasures washed overboard from passing sailboats.

How easy it is to enjoy life when the sky is blue and puffy clouds float in the heavens. Nature's beauty is there to thrill us every time – if we care to look.

Author Unknown

Sunsets

Like Folle Cove Beach, visit the beach at nightfall and delight in the surrounding beauty. A sunset bursts into the sky directly in front of you each night at sundown. You are rich! Spread out a blanket in the warm tropical evening, watch the sun fade to the purple night and listen to the orchestra of song from Coqui tree frogs in the nearby mangles. You won't be disappointed.

. . . .

Coquí is the common name for several species of small frogs. They are named for the very loud mating call which the males make at night. Males emit a two- part call consisting of a "co" which is used when threatened by another male and the "qui" which attracts females.

. . . .

Turtles

As elsewhere on the island, the green turtles and hawksbill turtles use the beach for nesting May through September. Turtle fences about 2 feet tall have been installed along the length of the beach to discourage turtles from crawling into road traffic on Route D 206. Like Folle Anse Beach, the area is protected by strict environmental rules enforced by the Department of Forestry. With wildflowers, shore birds, frogs, turtles and woods, it is nature at its best there on the beach for your environmental enjoyment.

A recent three-year study on Three Island Beach showed that hawksbill females vastly preferred laying their eggs in vegetated areas. About one-fifth of the nests were in the forest and most of the rest were in the forest border or in beach grass. Less than one-tenth were in open sand. Researchers found that both an open beach and a forest buffer (as exists on Three Island Beach) were ideal for reproducing a balanced hatching of male and female turtles. Eggs in the cooler forest shade 83° F (28.5° C) hatched mostly male turtles and those eggs on the beach and fringe with temperatures of 87° F (30.4° C) produced mostly females.

Port at Folle Anse

On the north end of the beach is Pointe de Folle Anse one of the 5 sea ports of Guadeloupe. Marie-Galante's port is used for exporting sugar products. This dock which extends several hundred feet into the water is a landmark which can be viewed from anywhere on the beach.

Three Islands Beach

BEACHSIDE RESTAURANTS

Some of Marie-Galante's beaches have snack bars and restaurants right on water's edge. Plan on visiting a different beach restaurant every day. Most are open for both lunch and dinner. Off-season they may be closed or have just evening hours, but during high season everything comes alive.

A variety of beach bars are there for you to explore. Some offer sunset viewing, others swimming, wading, entertainment, disco or a cozy, intimate and romantic setting. Still others offer floating tables and amazing views of the sea with back drop scenery of neighboring islands. A band or balladier will be playing somewhere on the island's beaches. Check out Chez Henri for island music. For boaters, dingy docking is available – after all, they are beach restaurants.

While each beach bar has its own unique personality, they all have one thing in common. All beat to the soothing rhythm of the breaking Marie-Galante waves.

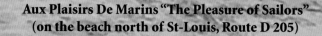

**Aux Plaisirs De Marins "The Pleasure of Sailors"
(on the beach north of St-Louis, Route D 205)**

SUN 7 Café - An Intimate Beachside Hideaway on Route D 203

Below is just a partial list of beachside bars and restaurants. Check them off as you visit them.

☐ Sun 7 (at Sunset Beach on D 203)

☐ Le Petit Anacardier (on the southern end of Feuillere Beach)

☐ Sacha (on Feuillere Beach)

☐ Le Reflet de I'lle (North of Feuillere Beach)

☐ Chez Henri (in downtown St-Louis)

☐ Le Wok (north of St-Louis on Route D 205)

☐ Aux Plaisirs De Marins (north of St-Louis on Route D 205)

☐ Le Touloulou (Route D 203 at the north end of Petite Anse)

☐ Le Skipper (in downtown St-Louis)

☐ Your Favorite _____

THE SECRETS OF MARIE-GALANTE'S BEACHES

"There's nothing more beautiful than the way the ocean refuses to stop kissing the shoreline, no matter how many times it's sent away."

Sarah Kay

The beautiful sandy beaches of Marie-Galante exist because of the "Goldilocks" circumstances of nature which bless the island – favorable waves and currents, fine coral sand, gradual beach slopes, coves and lagoons protected by off-shore reefs, – all are "just right" and ideal for the formation of magnificent beaches.

Let's begin with a look at the secret role waves play in the formation of these beaches.

Waves Are Awesome!

Whether small or large, waves are awesome to watch and experience. Pounding waves exploding onto the rocky shore are exciting, exhilarating and mesmerizing, while the smaller waves on a quiet sandy beach are soothing and relaxing. Just watching the waves and listening to the rhythm brings about a sense of peace.

Perhaps the most important reason beaches form are the waves. Beaches need waves. No waves, no beaches!

The size of the waves is determined by the strength of the wind, its duration and fetch (distance a wave travels). A strong wind blowing over hundreds of miles of ocean will create a more powerful wave than a weak wind blowing for just a few miles. The stronger the wind the greater the friction on the floor of the sea, and therefore the bigger the wave.

Some waves are low in height and have a long wave length. These are called low energy waves or "constructive waves" such as you normally see on the western shores of the island; beaches of Old Fort, Moustique, Canoe Cove, Mays, St-Louis, Folle Cove, and Three Islands. Waves here have a low frequency of between 6 and 8 waves per minute. Their wash carries fine particles of coral and shells up the beach to form a berm. The wave energy dissipates over a long area which results in a weak backwash. These small waves build high, wide summer beaches.

High energy waves are called "destructive waves." They have a large wave height and a short wave length. The frequency is high, between 13 and 15 waves per minute. The tall breakers have a high downward force and a strong backwash. Destructive waves that form during a storm may shrink the size of the beach. The larger the waves, the coarser the beach.

Large Atlantic waves which break over offshore reefs such as those on the eastern shore of the island, lose energy and are broken down to smaller waves which have a lower erosional impact on the beach. The roar of these breaking waves can be heard a mile away.

On Feuillere Beach, waves break obliquely to the shore creating longshore currents which transport sand along the shoreline. When the current confronts a barrier such as a groin on the northern end of the beach, the current loses energy and deposits the sand. Feuillere Beach, Petite Cove and the beaches of Grand-Bourg are protected by coral reefs off shore.

On Marie-Galante the difference between high and low tide is small (a maximum of 1.6 feet) when compared to tidal variations in other areas of the world, thus washout of the beach sand does not normally occur. These factors in combination with gentle beach slopes and the numerous coves and bays have resulted in the formation of sandy beaches, perfect for the emerald world where time has stopped.

Three major waves are found at the beach; *spilling waves, surging waves* and *plunging waves.*

Spilling waves are formed when a wave encounters a shallow sloping beach. The wave breaks over a long distance releasing its energy gradually over the near shore area of the beach. They provide enjoyment for boogie boarding and body rides as they roll and tumble to the beach. Generally, spilling waves are safer for children.

Surging waves occur in deeper water or between rocky and steep out-croppings. Swells passing abruptly from deep water to shallow water surge upward and flood forward, pushing swimmers into the steep shoreline. If the surge is large and the swimmer is near a rocky section of the shore, a surging wave can force the swimmer into the rocks.

Plunging waves or "surfers' waves" can be dangerous too. They peak and break all at once, sometimes forming an upper plunging lip and "pipeline" as they are called by surfers. In the "pipeline," air may be compressed and literally explode with a crack that adds drama to the rest of the wave's thunderous release of energy. All of the force of a plunging wave is dissipated in a small area. These are formed when large offshore waves suddenly encounter a sandbar, reef or an abrupt shallow (steep) beach. When a plunging wave breaks, it can pick up and pound a swimmer into the sand with great force, especially if it breaks on the shore. Experienced swimmers counteract these waves by diving into the base of the wave so as to slice through the wave without being overcome.

The energy of the wave depends on the height of the wave. As waves increase in height, the energy to be released increases by the height squared (h^2). Thus, a 3 foot wave is 9, not 3 times more powerful than a 1 foot wave. Waves over 5 feet in height can be dangerous, so unless you are an experienced surfer or water adventurer, avoid entering the water when the surf exceeds this threshold. For children even a 2 foot plunging wave can cause a tumble.

Waves are fun; fun to watch, fun for swimming and fun for board and kite surfing. Come to the beach and listen to the lapping of the ocean waves. They add a soothing and relaxing rhythm on the powder-white beaches.

. . . .

The tide is coming in and the swells are huge.
I imagine them rising from canyon depths somewhere beyond
the horizon and rolling endlessly, as they have been rolling for eons,
until they spend their pent-up energy crashing against the shore.

Richard Bode, Beachcombing at Miramar

. . . .

White Paradise Beaches

White Paradise Beaches

Just how were the powder-white paradise beaches of this emerald island formed, you may ask?

Mix small grains of coral, sea shells and limestone and you have the recipe for Marie-Galante's white sandy beaches. Up to 70% of the beach sand is made up of coral.

**Gibbus Parrotfish
(Scarus gibbus)
Courtesy NOAA**

Coral colonies have formed large reefs over many generations. While the coral is growing and adding to the size of the reef, it is also being eroded by grazing fish, invertebrates boring into the structure and the grinding by waves.

Parrotfish, urchins and other grazing ocean life play a major part in this "bio-erosion." The beautiful parrotfish spend their entire lives nibbling on dead coral with their sharp beak-like teeth. They don't feed off the coral per se; they eat the algae and micro-organisms living on it. In the nibbling process, small pieces of the hard coral are ingested. The fish can't metabolize the coral so the small "sand like" pieces pass through their digestive system where they are deposited as coral particles on the beach. At the same time the parrotfish beaks are kept clean and wear down to offset beak growth.

Without the help of grazers the coral would die. If you listen carefully the next time you go snorkeling you can actually hear them crunching as they bite and clean the coral surface.

One parrotfish can produce 100 kg (0.1 of a ton) of white sand every year. Thousands of parrotfish and the infinite measure of time have resulted in the spectaculaar beaches that we see today.

· · · · · · · · · · · · · · · · · · · ·

Sea urchins control seaweed and algae. They nibble away at the invasive seaweed and algae as it starts to grow, acting like underwater gardeners pulling weeds. They keep the invading seaweed and algae under control so the coral can thrive.

· · · · · · · · · · · · · · · · · · · ·

Seashells are the second ingredient of the "sand recipe." Shells, marine mollusks, barnacles, crabs, lobsters, brachiopods and skeletons of reef-living marine organisms are broken into small pieces by never ending waves. The shells are made of calcium carbonate, which is secreted by the outer surface of the mantle of the shell as the creature ages.

Rock is the final ingredient of beach sand. Small particles are eroded from the limestone bedrock which underlies the entirety of Marie-Galante. Limestone is particularly vulnerable to erosion. Cliffs on the northern shore are pounded by large waves formed over the eastern fetch of the ocean originating off the shores of continental Africa.

As these relentless waves erode the cliffs, large rocks fall away and into the sea. The sheer energy of the wave hitting the cliff causes these rocks to break down into smaller rocks. These in turn, are tossed about and ground into pebbles and ultimately to finer particles which become the other sand component of the beach. The very fine particles are deposited in the deeper waters while the courser particles are deposited on the shore.

What Is Coral?

Corals are tiny animals, or animal polyps in zoological terms. These marine invertebrates secrete calcium carbonate (limestone) to form a hard rock-like structure on the ocean floor. These underwater coral kingdoms are complex and stunningly beautiful.

Coral polyps have limited organ development and no central nervous system, but they do have a mouth surrounded by tentacles.

Hard (stony) corals found in the waters of Marie-Galante are reef-building corals. These coral polyps grow together into colonies of hundreds of thousands which are cemented together by the calcium carbonate they secrete. Living coral grows on top of the skeletons of their dead predecessors and in time builds up to form a reef.

Coralline red algae that grow upon and amidst the coral colonies and other invertebrate animals contribute to the building of a reef, but their contribution is small when compared to coral. The reef-building process is slow. Coral reefs are built over decades and centuries - not weeks or months.

There are about 20 different species of coral in the Caribbean, but not nearly as many as found in the Pacific, especially Australia where more than 300 different coral species have been identified. All coral forms are beautiful. In combination with the many unusual tropical fish that live in the reef, they provide a fascinating kaleidoscope of color for snorkelers.

. . . .

Why Are
The Waters Of Marie-Galante Beaches
A Pale Emerald Green?

The emerald color is distinctive to the coral beaches and reef system. The color is caused by the reflection of the blue sky, the shallow nutrient-free waters, water clarity and the white coral sands. They combine together to provide an emerald color that is found only on the tropical coral beaches and lagoons of the world.

. . . .

Shallow coral reefs grow best in salty warm water (70–85° F or 21–29° C). It is possible for soft corals to grow in places with warmer or colder water, but growth rates in these environments are very slow. Reef-building corals prefer clear and shallow water, low in nutrients with lots of sunlight. They grow best at depths shallower than 70 meters (230 ft). The most prolific reefs occupy depths of 18–27 meters (60–90 ft).

Warm tropical waters provide the perfect environment for coral life. Over decades, coral reefs have formed from Grand-Bourg to the beaches of Feuillard. The reefs provide a habitat for schools of fish of many kinds. The presence of these fish in combination with the coral result in the white sandy beaches and the glow of emerald blue waters that are the essence of Marie-Galante.

About 25% of the world's marine life lives around the coral reefs even though the reefs cover a small fraction (0.2%) of the ocean floor. Coral is so important to a healthy ecology that in the British Virgin Islands conservation groups are seeding (planting) staghorn and elkhorn coral in nurseries to restore damaged coral reefs.

. . . .

Coral reefs are vital to our beaches. Without them, there would be no white sandy beaches, no fish, no fishing, no jobs and no money.

Gerald Singer, Author, "St. John - Off The Beaten Track."

. . . .

Coral, Sponge and Seaweed Courtesy: National Marine Fishery Services of National Oceanic And Atmospheric Administration

Welcome To "The Coral Kingdom"

For those who have had the good fortune to view our planet from space, they are struck by the overwhelming impression that ours is a blue planet. Indeed over 70% of our planet is covered by water giving our home this blue aura. On closer inspection, patches of emerald and aquamarine become apparent in the larger expanse of deep blue. These patches are in the shallow waters of the tropics, fringing islands and the edges of continents; or, in turn, encircled by the ring-like islands that we call atolls.

Coming ever closer to Earth and approaching these oceanic jewels, a border of white is perceived which is revealed to be surf crashing against what appears to be a solid bastion of rock. Leaving our vantage point from above and diving into the sea, *we discover that what we think is solid rock is in fact a living mass - a kaleidoscopic vision of color, shape, and life that is a coral reef.*

Coral reefs are among the most amazing of ecosystems on our planet. Although found as solitary forms through 400 million years of geological history, the fossil record shows that corals evolved into modern reef-building organisms within the past 25 million years. Over those millions of years, coral reefs have evolved into the rainforests of the sea – a place of great biological diversity that is home to thousands of species that are found nowhere else. In fact, coral reefs are the most complex, species-rich, and productive of marine ecosystems.

Today, coral reefs, both modern and fossil, are studied as indicators of global change; as multi-faceted ecosystems with a plethora of species that could provide cures for forms of cancer and other ills afflicting mankind; and as highly endangered ecosystems that suffer from bleaching episodes related to warming of the global ocean, massive invasions of predatory species such as crown of thorns starfish, pollution from chemicals and sediment laden waters, and destructive fishing practices.

Because of their fragility, coral reefs have been compared to the proverbial "canary in the mine shaft" for the world ocean. Let us hope that we are able to preserve the beautiful creatures of the coral reefs and their wonderful ecosystems for future generations.

Courtesy: Coral Kingdom, Prepared By The US National Oceanic and Atmospheric Administration (NOAA)

. . . .

Enemies of the Coral Reefs

Because coral reefs grow very slowly, damage can take decades to repair. Snorkelers should not stand on the reefs. Boaters should not anchor over the reefs. Developers should prevent silt-laden construction runoff from reaching the waters. Turbidity will destroy the emerald world that is so special to Marie-Galante.

. . . .

Reefs Create Beaches

As large ocean waves pass over a coral reef their energy can be reduced by 75-95%, thus allowing the formation of calm sandy beach lagoons between the reef and the shore. To learn more about coral reefs, contact Endangered Species International (EIS) at www.endangeredspeciesinternational.org

. . . .

EXPLORE THE UNDERWATER WORLD

Beneath the waters at the timeless reefs of coral you will find the underwater emerald world of Marie-Galante. Here, there is a richness of life beyond imagination. The best way to see this world of fish, coral and plant life is by snorkeling.

Snorkelers Motto: Take only pictures; leave only bubbles.

Courtesy of The National Oceanic and Atmospheric Administration

If you haven't already been snorkeling, give it a try - you'll love the adventure, beauty, natural wonder and the spectacular display of aquatic life. Take pictures. Watch nature. Dive for junk. Identify species. There are fun things to do underwater.

An investment of 30 to 50 Euros for a snorkel, mask and fins is all that you need to get started. Rental of equipment will cost less -- about 10 Euros.

Try out your equipment. Float. Practice. Enjoy. The key to successful snorkeling is to relax. Start in the shallows where you can stand up. Lay face down in the water and begin to get comfortable breathing through the snorkel. Your skills will develop quickly as will your comfort and confidence. Soon you will be ready to explore the near-shore reefs and rocks. There are 500 different colorful tropical fish to find among the Caribbean reefs.

Mask

The secret to a successful snorkeling adventure is to have a mask that doesn't leak, or at least doesn't leak very much. Some leakage is inevitable.

Be sure to buy (or rent) a mask that fits your face. While holding the snorkel mask up to your face, breathe in through your nose. The mask should seal perfectly (without support from the strap or hands) and stay on for as long as you breathe in. If any air leaks in, water will also. Keep all hair out of the seal. For the best fit, the strap should fit snugly towards the top of the back of your head, not around your ears and back of your neck. If water does seep in while snorkeling, reach back and see if your strap has slipped down. Don't overly tighten the strap. If it is too tight the seal will be broken. The snorkel should rest in front of your ear. If the mask doesn't fit your face, try another before you buy. Once a mask that fits has been selected, the only way the mask will leak is if you exhale through your nose into the mask, or you laugh.

. . . .

Mask Tips

If your mask should be flooded with water it can be easily cleared by raising your head and pulling the lower edge of the mask away to break the seal and let the water drain out. Experienced snorkelers like to leave a little water in their mask where it can be swished around for an instant defog.

. . . .

Prescription lenses are an excellent investment and can be purchased along with the mask at many water sports stores. If renting, ask the store's sales personnel if they stock prescription masks. Many do.

Lens Fogging

Fogging of your mask must be prevented to ensure that you have the best underwater view. Fog is caused by condensation of water vapor due to a difference in temperature between the inside and outside of your mask. Your forehead can radiate enough heat to create instant fog. Likewise, your moist breath will cause fogging. Once a mask has fogged above water, it becomes more difficult to keep it from fogging up again during the dive.

When buying a new mask, it is important to read the manufacturer's instructions. Many mask lenses are coated with a protective film. Unless this film is removed, it's practically impossible to keep the mask from fogging during your dive. Before it is used, scrub the glass lens thoroughly with a cleanser. It might take more than one cleaning to completely remove the film.

Once the film has been removed, it is necessary to field treat the lens to prevent fogging while in use. A quick method of making your mask fog proof is to rub saliva (spit) on the inside of the mask lens. Rub the spit around with your finger until the lens is coated, then rinse it lightly. If spitting on your mask lens is undesirable, there are defogging products you can buy. The gel products work very well. Baby shampoo (a small drop) rubbed on the inside of the glass and then rinsed off with salt water can also help prevent fogging.

Snorkel

The snorkel is a plastic tube typically about 30 centimeters (1 ft) long and with an inside diameter of between 1.5 and 2.5 centimeters (0.6 and 1 inches). It is used for breathing air from above the water surface when your mouth and nose are submerged. The snorkel usually has a piece of rubber that attaches the snorkel to the outside of the strap of the mask. The mouthpiece swivels at the bottom of the snorkel riser so it can fit comfortably into your mouth while the riser end of the snorkel remains vertically above in the air. The swivel allows for adjustment. Put the mouthpiece all the way in your mouth and close your lips around it. Don't bite, just rest your teeth on the mouthpiece, otherwise your jaw will get sore.

· ·

Snorkel Tips

If your snorkel becomes flooded with water, a burst of air (similar to a dolphin blow, or by sharply blowing the word "two") should clear the water from the snorkel. Breathe in cautiously afterwards just to make sure.

If you're out of air, then simply remove the snorkel from the mouth to breathe. It's helpful to practice deliberately flooding and clearing both mask and snorkel to calmly learn these techniques.

· ·

Fins

Choose fins that fit properly; snug but not too tight. If the fins are too small, you may develop cramps in your toes and feet. If too large they may slip off. Remember they will slip on easier when your feet are wet.

Getting from the shore to the water wearing fins can be awkward. Like a lady entering a room, there is a graceful way, and then there is – well a graceless way. So it is with fins. We have all been amused by someone putting on their fins, duck-walking to the beach and splashing into the surf. The good news is there is a dignified way of doing this. Walk into the water with your fins in your hand until you are chest high in water, put on your mask and snorkel so you can see and breathe, then bend over to slip on you fins, just as you would put on your slippers.

Underwater Precautions

Almost all snorkeling accidents happen when people venture into deep water before they have practiced their skills in shallow water, especially the skill of clearing your mask and blowing water from the snorkel. Learn these skills, take your time, float when you get tired, don't touch the coral and stay within your physical fitness limits. For safety sake many snorkelers wear a buoyant foam-rubber wet suit or buoyancy vest. Above all, have a partner nearby to help in an emergency.

Stings from fire coral and cuts from sharp coral are the most common underwater injuries. It goes without saying that handling, prodding and exploring coral crevasse should be avoided.

Sea urchins (they look like black pin cushions or land mines) are found underwater at many beaches and likewise should be avoided. If you step on a prickly urchin the quill will cause a painful sting and may penetrate deeply into your flesh.

Other innocent-looking underwater animals that can sting include fire worms, Portuguese man-o-war, jellyfish and lionfish. If you are stung by a jellyfish don't panic, the sting is seldom fatal. Don't rub the injured area. Dab vinegar or rubbing alcohol on the injury. Later you can apply antihistamine cream.

· ·

If you are interested in identifying Caribbean reef fish, the best guide available is;

"Reef Fish Identification - Florida Caribbean Bahamas"
- 4th Edition by Paul Humann and Ned DeLoach.

· ·

TREASURES

"I believe there's no more wonderful world than the one waiting for me out there by the sea. An hour of beachcombing, of strolling through the silky sand with the sun at my back and the endless blue horizon melting before me, calms my mind as it invigorates my body. I always return home the better for it with lungs full of fresh air and pockets full of interesting things."

S. Deacon Riatterbush, "A Beachcombers Odyssey."

A beach is a place of discovery; a place to find beauty, solitude, "things" that wash up on the shore, lost treasures and antiquities. Most of all it is a place to discover the joy of being alive.

Everything on a beach tells a story. Interpreting this story and wondering about the history of the treasure is the most interesting part of the exploration.

As Columbus discovered, the gold of the Caribbean is not found in the island hills but in the early morning sun on the beaches -- golden beaches. So visit them. Visit them when no one else is there; alone. Watch the sun come up with the mist shining in multi colors through the morning landscape, over the white sands and emerald waters of Marie-Galante.

Begin your day with "beach music" – the soothing rhythm of lapping waves and the call of the gulls, a call that pleads for you to breathe deeply the sweet fragrance of life – the flowers, the salt air, open sea and warm breeze.

"I have never found a companion that was as companionable as solitude."
Henry David Thoreau

The Treasure Solitude

Bask in the quiet solitude – oh the precious solitude. Gain inspiration from the birds, fish and creatures, for in this moment of solitude they are your only beach companions.

Things on the Beach

. . . .

Doubting that they would ever find land, Columbus noticed,
here drifting in the sea, "a man-made plank, carved by an unknown hand,
perhaps with an iron tool," then "a little wax candle bobbing up and down,"
both clear signs that land and humanity were nearby.

Laurence Bergreen, Historian

. . . .

Since the beginning of time, all sorts of curiosities have floated in the ocean and washed up on the beaches. These are the "things" searched for by every beachcomber. They may be shells, sea glass, driftwood, things lost overboard, pottery chards, arrow heads, artifacts, fishing nets, valuables and useless marine things, debris and trash.

For the beachcomber most of the man-made flotsam can be collected, but removal of seashells from the beach is prohibited. Rather than remove the shell, take a picture of beautiful and unusual shells that you may wish to remember, or visit the local gift shop and purchase market-legal shells that you have discovered.

While out on adventure, good ethics calls for us to pick up trash that we may find. If you do, you will leave the beach more beautiful and safer than it was when you got there.

Good ethics also calls for protecting wildflowers and wildlife such as starfish, crabs, fish, turtles and nests. All of God's creature should be photographed but left on the beach. Some beachcombers carve messages in the sand, build a cairn (piles of stones to mark a trail), make sand castles and beach shelters. Go ahead make a sand angel. Write a love letter in the sand. It's OK to have fun.

. . . .

"An early morning walk is a blessing for the whole day."
Henry David Thoreau

. . . .

Checklist For The Beach Quest

Footwear & Gloves - To get the most out of your experience, wear good beach footwear. Flip flops will suffice, but old sneakers, beach booties or felt bottomed scuba booties provide better protection against sharp objects, plus they grip slippery surfaces. Lightweight gloves are nice when picking around debris.

Sun Protection - Don't forget to bring sunglasses, sun screen, a hat and a light-weight shirt. Protective clothing is essential. If you have fair skin, the tropical sun will burn your skin in a half hour.

Camera - Shells and so much more can be captured with your camera. A camera on a neck strap is ideal and always handy.   Don't place it in your shirt pocket because it will drop into the water the first time you bend over to pick up a treasure.

Containers - Bring bags, one plastic disposable bag for trash pickup, a canvas bag or light-weight backpack and perhaps a handy zip lock bag to store the little treasures you find on the beach.

Reference Book - If you have room, bring your species identification book and a pencil and note paper.

Metal Detectors

For the serious minded beachcomber, you may wish to enjoy exploring for buried treasure with a metal detector. Gerry McMullen who has searched for buried treasure throughout the world provides tips for finding treasures buried in the sands.

Objects found with a metal detector come when you least expect it, so take a lighthearted approach relax and enjoy doing something you love. It may take a little time but if you stick with it, you will eventually find a special object hidden in the powder-white sands of Marie-Galante.

Even if your quest yields nothing, walk the shoreline anyway. Do it without a care for finding a shell or treasure, do it to refresh your spirit and soul. That's what makes us feel alive, bringing us back again and again. Every day on the beach is a gift, regardless of the yield.

Sun Shelter Built by Beachcombers on Feuillard Beach

Driftwood Art Found on the Beach

. . . .

Treasures With A Metal Detector
Tips from Gerry McMullen

You won't get rich beachcombing with a metal detector but you may be surprised at what you will discover. Who knows, maybe an artifact from antiquity. In the course of 6 hours there is a good chance you will find something of value, most likely a few pieces of jewelry and coins. *My personal best is 5 gold rings!* At resorts, ask about any reported lost items on the beach. Returning valuables to the owner whenever possible is the right thing to do and it brings good Karma.

Beach selection is critical. Highly used beaches at expensive resorts are best for finding valuable jewelry. About 95% of jewelry is lost in the wading zone from the knees to the waist. The remote beaches of Marie-Galante are not going to be as productive as the resort beaches of Puerto Rico or the "umbrella fields" of St. Martin. Because the tidewaters on Marie-Galante only fluctuates a foot or so, the scour area (the prime area of discovery) is not very large.

The best time to go out is early in the morning before everyone shows up. Exploring the newly exposed beach at low tide and after a storm can be productive.

Don't forget the sunbathing area of the beach. It doesn't take much to lose a nice wrist watch or the hand-crafted bottle opener that was purchased at the local gift shop the day before.

Regarding metal detection equipment, there are many good ones. I have had great satisfaction in salt water with the Minelab Excalibur, CTX 3030 and Fisher CZ-21.

Enjoy your treasure exploration! For more information on metal detection hunts and training visit: www.gerrysdetectors.com.

. . . .

It's not a competition. You may look down the shore one day and see other beachcombers. Be friendly with them and exchange information. Find out what they are looking for. They may be hunting for valuables; you may be searching for the sake of discovery. Keep in mind, this is your hunt. You're in this for your own unique rewards.

A VERY
SPECIAL ISLAND

SUGARCANE

Livestock and sugarcane are major sources of income for local farmers on Marie-Galante. It is common throughout the island to see cattle and goats staked out in a meadow for grazing. Fencing is not commonly practiced. Livestock are sold at the local markets on Guadeloupe.

By far the more significant agricultural product is sugarcane. About 6500 acres (2650 hectares) of cane fields provide sugar for the Grande Anse Refinery (Usine de Grande-Anse) and three local distilleries (Bellevue, Bielle, and Poisson). While there has been a 50% decline in sugarcane production in the past 20 years, sugarcane is still "king" in this remote area of the Caribbean.

The "Sugar Knowledge International Limited" (SKIL) (www.sucrose.com) provides an excellent explanation of the role of the sugarcane crop on Marie-Galante.

The sugar content for mature cane is about 10% by weight but the figure depends on the variety, the season and location. One hectare (2.47 acres) of sugarcane can grow 100 tons of cane or 10 tons of sugar per hectare.

Cane Farmer Returning from Sugar Factory

Growing the Cane

Sugarcane is a tall perennial grass that thrives in sub-tropical and tropical climates. It prefers lots of sun and water but the roots do not like to be waterlogged. A cane takes about 12 months to reach maturity although the time varies widely around the world from as short as 8 months to 24 months. It differs from many crops in that it re-grows from the roots and provides a crop for several years before it peters out. Typically the canes get shorter and shorter until at 6 to 10 years it is time to replant using genetically improved high-yield and disease resistant varieties. Over 600 different varieties exist.

Canes are harvested by chopping down the stems and taking them to the factory by truck or ox-drawn cart (cabrouets.) While manual harvesting of the canes by machete is still practiced, the sugarcane industry is moving rapidly to mechanize harvesting.

· · · · · · · · · · · · · · · · · · · ·

Once cut, sugarcane is highly perishable and needs to be processed at the mill as soon as possible to avoid losing its sugar content. Most crops are delivered to a mill less than 24 hours after harvesting.

· · · · · · · · · · · · · · · · · · ·

Producing Sugar

Extraction - The first stage of processing is the extraction of the cane juice. Cane is cut into small pieces and crushed using a series of large rollers. The rollers work just like the small wringers used on domestic washing machines a century ago. Sweet juice is pressed out of the canes and brought to boilers. The juice contains soil from the fields, small cane fiber and other impurities which must be separated from the sugar.

Evaporation - The soil and impurities in the juice are removed with slaked lime (a relative of chalk) and returned to the fields to grow another crop. Once this is done, the juice is boiled in an evaporator and thickened into syrup. Sometimes the syrup is cleaned of impurities again.

Boiling - In the last stage, the syrup is placed in a very large pan and boiled until it is transformed into sugar crystals. In the factory the workers may have to throw in sugar dust to initiate crystal formation. Once the crystals have grown, the resulting mixture of crystals and mother liquor is spun in centrifuges to separate the two. The crystals are then dried with hot air before being stored in bulk bins.

Storage - The final raw sugar forms a sticky brown mountain in the bin and looks like the soft brown sugar used for cooking. It could be used like that but it still has some impurities and an unpleasant taste. This is addressed through refinement after it is shipped to the destination country. With the residual sugar juice that did not crystallize, a sweet by-product of molasses is made. This may be turned into cattle food or sent to a distillery where alcohol (rum) and ethanol are made.

Power

So what happened to all that fiber from crushing the sugarcane? It is called "bagasse" in the industry. The factory needs electricity and steam to run the process machinery. The bagasse is burnt in large furnaces where the heat is used to boil water and make high pressure steam. The steam is then used to drive turbines to make electricity and to operate the factory. Thus, the entire raw cane is used or recycled in the sugar making process.

WINDMILLS

Imagine the slow pace of life 150 years ago when every small plantation had their own mill. Early in the history of Marie-Galante, animals were used to power the mills. Oxen circled to turn the mill shaft. Mangles (crushing rollers or wringers) squeezed juice from the sugarcane or ground up the grain. Cane juice was collected beneath the rollers and drained to boiling house tanks positioned nearby and downhill.

Oxen did not live very long, so in the 17th century planters turned to horses and cattle to conduct this burdensome work. Where there was a constant breeze from the ocean such as is characteristic of all of Marie-Galante, windmills were constructed. They worked faster than animal mills. Sails (windmill blades) would capture the wind's energy and turn the shaft to continue the relentless grinding by the mill.

Mills were typically 30 feet tall, conical in shape and made of stone walls 3 feet in thickness capable of carrying the heavy load of the turning sails. Some had a wooden cap that could be swiveled by a large boom to face the day's wind.

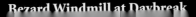

Bezard Windmill at Daybreak

The huge spinning sail blades rotated a horizontal shaft. A bevel gear or miter gear converted the horizontal shaft to a vertical shaft which reached to the floor where the milling occurred. Slaves fed vertical crushers with fresh cut sugarcane received by the cartload from field crews. Any delay and the juice in the cane might ferment and spoil.

Historian Dr. Grant Cornwell reports, "There was no stopping the mill. This was profoundly dangerous work; on the wall of each mill hung an ax to chop off the arm of a slave who got caught in the crushers."

In the confines of the boiler room where slaves kept fires to boil and concentrate the syrup, it was hell in a tropical environment where it was hot just sitting in the shade.

. . . .

"If a Mill-feeder be catch'd by the finger, his whole body is drawn in, and is squees'd to pieces, If a Boyler gets any part into the scalding Sugar, it sticks like Glew, or Birdlime, and 'tis hard to save either Limb or Life."

Cited in Bridenbaugh and Bridenbaugh 1972, 301

. . . .

It is hard to imagine this harsh world of years past.

Over 100 mills were constructed on Marie-Galante, 70 of which are still standing as ruins.

Today, only 1 mill remains and operates on a daily basis. About a kilometer from the Bellevue Distillery, the windmill at the Bezard Estate has been renovated and now can be seen crushing cane. When you get to Marie-Galante don't miss seeing this mill in action. The mill is in operation daily between 11:00 AM and 2:00 PM (14:00 local time.)

MOONRISES

Guillarmo Gomez Gil, Courtesy Bridgeman Art Library

"You are here.
The moon tides are here.
And that's all that matters."

Sanober Khan

Marie-Galante is the perfect place for romance. When a tropical breeze, a white-washed sandy beach and moon-glow combine together, a magical moment is born. It doesn't take a full moon to catalyze that moment. Any bright moonlit night will do on this paradise island. However there are special nights. *Each month on Marie-Galante just after the sun sets in the west, a full moon rises on the horizon of the east.* Lose yourself in the moonlight. Share the moon dust of this moment with someone special. They belong to you for the night.

SPECIAL MOONRISE NIGHTS
Between 7:00** & 8:00 PM

| | YEAR | |
MONTH	2017	2018
January	13	3*
February	12	1
March	13	2
April	12	30
May	11	30
June	10	28
July	9	28
August	8	27
September	7	26
October	7	26
November	5	24
December	5*	24

* Super Moon- on this date the moon is closest to the earth and is therefore 7% bigger and 30% brighter than usual.
** Approximate time for full moon rising

To see the "mistress of the night" as she gradually rises and casts her wonderment of shadows and mystery, romantics go to Capesterre and beaches on the east – Petite Cove and Feuillere Beach or to the remote beaches of Taliseronde and Feuillard. A beach blanket, glass of wine and tender words add to this magic of the emerald world where time has stopped.

And if a rain shower should begin somewhere in the distance as the moon rises, look for a **moonbow.** *Yes there is such a thing,* a display of rainbow colors created by the light of the moon.

. . . .

Like love, the moon holds the answers to questions man has yet learned to ask.

Author Unknown

. . . .

And what about moonsets you may wonder. Are there full moonsets too? Well, yes. However, the angels wouldn't allow such melancholy of a setting moon to conclude a day in paradise. Moonsets happen just before day break. Shortly after the full moon sets and the beach momentarily settles into darkness, the sun rises on the eastern horizon – setting the sky afire – a gift from the angels of another beautiful day. That is just the way it is in the "Goldilocks" world of Marie-Galante.

. . . .

You can find your own special moments at; www.timeanddate. com/. Click on sunsets or moonrise for Guadeloupe. For information on the science of moonrises visit the Lunar and Planetary Institute website at: www.lpi.usra.edu/

. . . .

Moon Pictures

If you are a photographer, shooting the moon can result in excellent pictures. The best time is during twilight as a full moon is rising while the sun is setting – the "golden hour." Choose a time when the colors of the sky are rich and surroundings are visible. Explore using a fast shutter speed to under expose the moon which makes the moon the focal point of the picture. Play with settings to get the perfect shot.

SUNRISES & SUNSETS

SUNRISES & SUNSETS

*Few sunrises are greeted as eagerly as those viewed
through the eyes of love.*

Author Unknown

A sea which disappears on the horizon and an approaching twilight means there is a beautiful sunrise and sunset virtually every day on the emerald island of Marie-Galante.

Every sunset is beautiful, but sunsets with high clouds of red, pink and purple pierced by the rays of the setting sun are spectacular. For these special gifts of the heavens, don't miss romantic sunset strolls on St-Louis Beach, Three Island Beach, and the shores of Moustique Beach. As for sunrises, watch the dawning sun rise each day at Feuillere, Feuillard and Taliseronde beaches.

How long does it take for the sun to set?

Answer: The diameter of the sun is 0.5 degrees and the sun moves 15 degrees an hour (360 / 24) so the sun sets in 1/30 of an hour or two minutes. This marks the onset of twilight.

It only takes 2 minutes from the time the bottom of the sun reaches the horizon to the time the top of the sun sinks below the horizon (sunset time). Don't worry about the math; just remember that the sky is spectacular a half hour before sunset and the 25 minutes of afterglow following sunset. This afterglow is called the "blue hour," a time when the sky "afire" announces the blue of the night and heavens of starlight. It is called *l'heure bleue* by the islanders.

Breathe in and live in the richness of the moment, because it belongs to you and you alone. So look up the sunrise and sunrise times. Head to the beaches and plan for a spectacular Marie-Galante sky.

"— spectacular shades of scarlet, orange, and red most often grace cirrus and altocumulus layers, but only rarely low clouds such as stratus or stratocumulus. When low clouds do take on vivid hues, as they often do over the open ocean in the tropics, it is a clue that the lower atmosphere is very clean and therefore more transparent than usual."

Stephen F. Corfidi, NOAA/NWS Storm Prediction Center

SUNRISES AND SUNSETS ARE FREE
Every Morning and Every Night

MONTH	Sunrise* AM	Sunset* (Military Time)
January	6:38	17:53
February	6:32	18:09
March	6:14	18:16
April	5:53	18:21
May	5:31	18:23
June	5:28	18:32
July	5:36	18:36
August	5:46	18:27
September	5:52	18:07
October	5:58	17:46
November	6:10	17:34
December	6:26	17:36

15th day of each month

Green Flash - Have you heard of the "green flash?" Just as the last bit of sun sets below the ocean horizon, a flash of green occurs. Look carefully, the green flash lasts for only a few seconds. You must have an ocean horizon for the green flash to be observed.

· · · · · · · · · · · · · · · · · · · ·

Green flashes are real (not illusory) phenomena seen at sunrise and sunset, when some part of the sun suddenly changes color (at sunset, from red or orange to green or blue).

The word "flash" refers to the sudden appearance and brief duration of this green color, which usually lasts only a second or two.

· · · · · · · · · · · · · · · · · · · ·

Hawksbill Turtles

Hawksbill turtles are indigenous to Marie-Galante. They are the most colorful and beautiful turtles of all. Unlike other sea turtles, they avoid the open ocean, spending their time in coral reefs, rocks, lagoons, mangroves and coastal shallows. They feed almost exclusively on sponges with a secondary diet of shrimp, squid and other invertebrates. Named for their sharp bird-like beak, hawksbills can reach into cracks and crevices of coral reefs looking for food.

These turtles are solitary, nesting in low densities on quiet Caribbean beaches such as Marie-Galante's Three Island Beach and Taliseronde Beach. From May to October turtles come ashore to lay eggs which have been fertilized by several male suitors in the prior days and months. It is not uncommon for a nest to have a clutch of eggs fertilized by more than 1 suitor. Adult females are well adapted for crawling over reefs and rocks to reach preferred nesting areas. The hawksbill, like all sea turtles, travels hundreds and even thousands of miles across the ocean to the sands from which they hatched 20 to 30 years before. Simply finding the same location let alone finding the same beach is remarkable. They will return again every year that they nest, for decades, until they die.

US Fish and Wildlife Service SE Region

Females may nest 3 to 5 times per season at 2 week intervals and lay up to 140 eggs per nest, usually at night. A pit is dug in the sand, filled with eggs, and then covered. At this stage the female turtle returns to the sea, leaving the eggs to hatch on their own. Two months later in the dark of night 72% to 92 % of the eggs will hatch. The small new-born turtles scamper to the water attempting to reach the safety of the ocean before daylight when they become visible pray for gulls, land crabs and other predators. It is estimated that only 1 in 1000 turtles survive to adulthood.

Size/Longevity - Adults weigh between 100-200 pounds (45 - 90 kg) and reach 2-3 feet (roughly 0.5 to 1 meter) in length. They may live for 30 to 50 years although little scientific information is known of their life expectancy.

Endangered Species - The hawksbill is categorized as a critically endangered species. Their population has declined more than 80% in the last century. People around the world still eat sea turtle eggs despite the turtle's international protection status. They are often killed for their flesh despite the fact that toxins from sponges which the turtle eats accumulate in their tissue and may be poisonous to humans. These graceful sea turtles are also drowned when entangled in commercial fishing nets. Discarded ropes, tackle and fish hooks all add to their struggle for life.

Historically their stunning shells have been used for making jewelry, combs and other novelties. Despite the fact that the international trade of their shells is illegal, there is still a thriving black market. When purchasing tortoise souvenirs, be sure you are buying synthetic materials for it is illegal to trade, purchase or possess sea turtle products.

The highway along Trois Ilets (Three Island) Beach borders one of the island's important nesting sites. Although there is a 150 foot vegetated buffer between the water and the highway, many turtles crawl onto the road and are run over by vehicles. In an effort to prevent this from happening, conservationists have built turtle barricades–fences woven out of woodland brush about 2 feet tall.

Green Sea Turtles

Green sea turtles also use Marie-Galante beaches for nesting. These turtles are among the largest in the world; much larger than the hawksbill. They may weigh up to 450 pounds. Their proportionally small head, which is not retractable, extends from a heart-shaped shell of armor that measures up to 4 feet (1.5 meters) in length. It is named not for the color of its shell, which is brown or olive depending on its habitat, but for the greenish color of its skin.

While most sea turtles warm themselves by swimming close to the surface of shallow waters, the green turtle will take to land to bask in the sun. While different from hawksbills in size and color, their nesting habits are nearly the same. Every two to four years green turtles undertake lengthy migrations from feeding sites to nesting grounds, the same beach used by their mothers. Mating with one or more males takes place in shallow waters close to the shore. To nest, females leave the sea, dig a cavity, lay their eggs, then return to the sea leaving the eggs to incubate and hatch on their own.

As with the hawksbill turtle, the green turtle is listed as an endangered species.

Courtesy of Doug Helton, NOAA/NOS/ORR/ERD

Other Sea Turtles

Of the 7 known sea turtle species in the world (leatherback, green, loggerhead, kemp's ridley, hawksbill and olive ridley), 4 have been identified as "endangered" or "critically endangered" with another two being classed as "vulnerable." The kemp's ridley and hawksbill turtles are listed as "critically endangered," the loggerhead and green as "endangered," the olive ridley and leatherback as "vulnerable." There is not enough information on the flatback turtle to determine their conservation status.

The loggerhead and the leatherback visit the waters and islands of the West Indies but they spend much of their lives in the open sea. Both the loggerhead and the leatherback are very large turtles with the leatherback being the largest of all. In 1988 a 2019 pound leatherback turtle was found washed up dead on the shores of Wales. The olive ridley is found mostly in the pacific waters from Mexico to Costa Rica and India.

Sea turtles are prehistoric, having roamed the earth for millions of years. Although the leatherback grows to over 2000 pounds, Archelon an extinct turtle which roamed the seas 80 million years ago was even bigger, measuring more than 4 meters (13 ft) long, and about 4.9 meters (16 ft) wide from flipper to flipper. The freshwater turtle Stupendemys is reported to have been even bigger.

For more information on Marie-Galante's turtles visit: www.sea turtles.org or donate to protect the sea turtles at; www.savetheseaturtle.org. Also visit the NOAA site: http://www.nmfs.noaa.gov/pr/species/turtles/.

. . . .

Terms to describe the turtle population health

Extinct: All of that specie is gone and no more are left to be seen.

Critically Endangered: The species has a very high risk of being extinct throughout all or a significant portion of its range.

Endangered: The species is in danger but not very soon.

Vulnerable: The species is not endangered yet but the numbers are dropping continuously.

Threatened: The species is likely to become an endangered species within the foreseeable future throughout all or a significant portion of its range.

. . . .

Turtle Facts

- An adult hawksbill turtle eats an average of 1200 lbs (544 kg) of sponges a year!

- Hawksbills are capable of nesting faster than any other species of sea turtle. They complete the entire process in less than 45 minutes.

- Turtles typically hold their breath underwater for 3 to 30 minutes, but large leatherback turtles can remain submerged for 60 to 70 minutes.

- Large leatherback turtles have been known to dive to a depth of 3,900 feet, but the green, loggerhead, hawksbill, olive ridley and kemp's ridley sea turtles usually dive to a depth of 150 to 900 feet.

- The sex of a sea turtle is determined by the temperature of the nest. Those located in the open sun typically hatches females while cooler nests in the shade produces males. A nesting temperature over 91^0 F can result in turtle deformities.

- Hatchlings wait until darkness to scramble from the nest, then head toward the light of the ocean horizon to find water and their ultimate home. Artificial lights from porches, street lights and automobiles can disorient new borns and cause them to lose their way where they may be eaten by predators.

- Turtles can travel at a speed of 1 mile per hour or more. Since they may travel in a straight line to a distant feeding destination, a turtle will travel more than 24 miles in a day. A leatherback which is a born traveler will cover more than 75 miles in 1 day.

- Fishing tackle and ropes entangle turtles. They are the leading cause of injury. If snared in a net and held under water, a turtle will drown.

- In 1492 Christopher Columbus reported the following in his log; "In those twenty leagues...the sea was thick with turtles...so numerous that it seemed the ships would run aground on them —." Today, these populations have declined 95%.

- Loggerheads and leatherback turtles roam the oceans from Newfoundland to Trinidad and beyond. When they mature at 25 to 35 years, female turtles will return to the beach from which they were born and lay a hundred or more fertile eggs in 4 to 8 different nests spread over the 6 to 8 week nesting season. No one knows just how they are able to find their way home after such a long journey.

On display at the Yale Peabody Museum

Endangered or Threatened Marine Turtles[1]

Species	Status	Adult Weight	Adult Shell Length	Lifespan
Kemp's Ridley	Endangered	- 100 pounds - Smallest sea turtle	24-28 inches	Unknown
Green Turtle	Endangered & threatened	140 to 450 pounds	Up to 4 feet	-Unknown. Perhaps 60 yrs. -Sexual maturity at 25 to 40 yrs.
Hawksbill Turtle	Endangered	100-150 pounds	25-35 inches	Unknown
Leatherback Turtle	Endangered	Up to 2,000 pounds	6.5 feet	-Unknown -Perhaps 150 years
Loggerhead Turtle	Endangered & threatened	175-440 pounds	3 to 4 feet	-Unknown - Sexual maturity at around 35 years old

[1] Courtesy of NOAA See http://www.nmfs.noaa.gov and "Sea Turtles," by James R. Spotila

[2] Turtle art work: courtesy of J. C. ParkerFineArt.com

Diet	Range	Appearance	Nesting Practice
Crabs, fish, jellyfish, and mollusks	Gulf of Mexico/SE Coast of US	- Grayish-green, nearly circular, top shell -Pale yellowish bottom shell	Nesting occurs in herds ie. together with many other Ridleys. This is called "amibadas."
-Herbivorous -Sea grasses and algae	Globally distributed in tropical and subtropical waters between 30° North and 30°South of the equator.	-Shell is smooth with shades of black, gray, green, brown and yellow -The turtle bottom is yellowish white.	-Females return to the beaches where they were born ("natal" beaches). -Eggs are laid in summer months every 2-6 years.
- Sponges & other invertebrates - Algae	Hawksbill turtles live in tropical and subtropical water between 30° N to 30° S latitude. They are widely distributed throughout the coral beaches of the Caribbean sea.	-Top serrated shell is dark to golden brown, with streaks of orange, red, and/or black. -Bottom shell (plastron) is clear yellow	-Females return to natal beaches every 2-3 years. -A new nest will be laid every 14-16 nights during the nesting season. -They commonly nest on pocket beaches with little or no sand.
Soft-bodied animals, such as jellyfish salps, and pyrosomes	They roam over the world except arctic and Antarctic.	-Black shell with white splotches -Pinkish-white belly	Females lay clutches of approximately 100 eggs several times during a nesting season at 8-12 day intervals.
Whelks and conch	Loggerheads occur throughout the temperate and tropical regions of the world.	-Reddish-brown, slightly heart-shaped top shell -Pale yellow bottom shell	Females nest from April-September. They have 3-5 nests per season.

ISLAND LIFE BEFORE COLUMBUS

Columbus's discovery long, long, ago profoundly changed the life of the native islanders of the Caribbean Sea. For these simple people, he and the exploiters that followed brought a cruel wave of enslavement, disease, death and extinction that washed over the thousands of Caribbean islands, including the small island of Marie-Galante.

Recorded history on Marie-Galante is limited, but island life here in paradise was probably no different from other islands in the Caribbean Sea.

The story of early life was taken from the journals of Christopher Columbus and other explorers of the time. It begins on an island somewhere in the Bahamas, probably San Salvador.

It was Friday October 12, 1492. The very air trembled with awe, fear and magic when 3 ships appeared on the horizon of the Caribbean. Imagine the excitement that erupted from the native people gathered on the white powdery beaches and in the villages. Who were these explorers dressed so strangely in a way never seen before, with steel swords that could cut your hand in an instant; and those muskets that brought forth thunder from above? And where did these magnificent ships with tall masts and white sails come from?

As the sun rose on October 12, the presence of Christopher Columbus, Admiral of the Ocean Sea filled the air. Men, women and children shouted to their neighbors, "Come! Come! Come see the men from the sky," as if Columbus and his sailors were from the very heavens, sent by God.

. . . .

Columbus and his voyagers were equally in awe of this new world. He recorded that he may have discovered the entrance to paradise.

. . . .

The natives were marvelous swimmers and canoeists. Upon seeing the ships anchored three miles off shore, natives swam the distance to greet these strange people and see first-hand these wonders "from the sky."

The very first night, Columbus wrote in his journal that the islands were very heavily populated by a handsome, strong, well-built and peaceful people who had only simple weapons. The people were gentle and religious. They were generous particularly with their food. All shared. Columbus was impressed with the cleanliness of the villages.

His journals say much about the dark desire and motivation of the explorers. Columbus reports that with as few as 50 of his men and their advanced weapons, he could take over the islands. Almost immediately, Columbus took several native boys aboard his ship to seek information on the location of gold. In his first two weeks his journals mention gold 70 times.

What follows describes life on this Friday October 12, 1492, the day that Columbus discovered this emerald world that he thought was paradise. It was a day that would change the lives of the native people forever.

At the time of Columbus, many of the 3000 Caribbean islands were inhabited by hundreds of thousands, perhaps even several million native Caribbeans. They belonged to two major tribes, the Tainos and Caribs. The Tainos lived primarily in the Greater Antilles, the islands of today's Cuba, Haiti, Dominican Republic, Puerto Rico and Jamaica. Caribs lived in the Lesser Antilles, the smaller southern islands. Marie-Galante is one of these smaller southern islands.

. . . .

The word Antilles (or Antilia) is a medieval term used by explorers to define unexplored and mysterious lands featured on their charts.

. . . .

As sea-faring skills developed in South America centuries before Columbus, adventuring natives began the exploration and settlement of the islands just 100 to 500 miles off their mainland. They hollowed out huge trees to form long dugout canoes with flat bottoms. The canoes were finely worked by alternately charring and chopping the canoe cavity using stone axes (celts). One such canoe was later measured by Columbus to be 96 feet long with an 8 feet beam. With these canoes, families migrated to the islands bringing with them dogs, agouti (small hamster-like rodents), ceramics, and mainland garden plants. They also brought root crops and other materials needed for settlement. These Indian settlers were clever, ingenious and had everything they needed to survive.

Since many of the islands were visible from one to the other, it was natural that these new visitors would explore and populate the islands – first one, then the next and the next for over 1000 miles throughout the island chain. Families set down roots where fresh water and fertile soils were available. Villages formed, some contained thousands of people. The ocean that surrounded these islands was both a barrier and highway. It provided a water barrier of protection against invaders but also a waterway for trade and for forming and strengthening alliances.

Villages were defended with bows and arrows with fire-hardened tips, wooden spears, heavy wooden war clubs called a macana, blowguns with darts tipped in poison, spear-throwing slings and stone hatchets.

Natives had no knowledge of metallurgy and thus did not use iron, steel, bronze or copper for tools and weapons. Baskets, ceramic bowls and gourds were used for carrying and storing food and water. Stones, sea shells and turtle shells were shaped into fish hooks and axes. Tools were made for grinding cassava into flour, cutting up fish and for completing other chores. Fish nets and sleeping hammocks were woven using cotton from local plants. All needs were met in these simple ways. Life was good. Life was aligned with the rhythms of nature.

Shelters were often round, constructed of wood with thatched roofs of straw and palm leaves, each housing a family or clan with the capacity to accommodate 30 members or more. Christopher Columbus's journal notes that the thatched homes "could not be more graceful nor better made, more secure, cleaner nor healthier."

Social order among the Tainos was established by chiefs who set forth guidelines by which all tribe members lived. They hunted, fished, cultivated crops and ate the abundant fruits provided by nature. They had beautiful ceremonies that were held at various times – birth, death, marriage, harvest, to name a few. They had special reverence for the "Earth Mother" (Atabey) and had respect for life, believing that all living things are connected.

. . . .

What is Cassava?

Cassava is the third largest source of carbohydrates in the tropics. It was a major staple for the Caribbean native people. It is one of the most drought-tolerant crops, capable of growing on marginal soils.

Cassava contains toxins. Improper preparation of cassava can leave enough residual cyanide to cause acute cyanide intoxication, goiters, and even ataxia or partial paralysis.

One of the traditional ways to prepare bitter cassava roots is by first peeling and grating the roots, and then prolonged soaking of the gratings in water to allow leaching and fermentation to take place, followed by thorough cooking to release the volatile hydrogen cyanide gas. Cutting the roots into small pieces, followed by soaking and boiling in water is particularly effective in reducing the cyanide content in cassava.

Caribbean islanders understood the importance of soaking and squeezing out the toxins in cassava. Bread made from cassava is very tasty.

Source: Wikipedia

. . . .

There was little need for clothing due to the very favorable climate and so the natives were mostly naked "as their mother bore them" described Columbus. Young adults were considered to be old enough for marriage when they entered puberty. After marriage, women wore small woven skirts or aprons for privacy. The men remained naked.

Caribs, admired and feared as brave and fierce warriors, were willing to paddle their war canoes (50 or more men to a canoe) long distances to capture wives on nearby islands, thus ensuring a growing or stable population and a diverse gene pool. In Carib communities, the bravest warriors provided island leadership in place of tribal chiefs as was the custom in the Taino culture.

The fierceness of Caribs and their reputation as man-eating warriors caused fear in the hearts of potential enemies. Ominously painted in black, red or white, Carib warriors were frightening. They believed that by eating the bravest of those who fell in battle, they would gain the qualities of the brave defeated warrior. Their reputation as cannibals was a legendary deterrent and warning to those who might have been tempted to invade their island homelands.

The Caribs led a relatively easy life on their paradise islands where the climate was just about perfect - food was abundant - clams, land crabs, turtles, turtle eggs, fish of all sorts, farm crops of manioc (yucca, cassava) and maize which was used for baking unleavened bread. Fruit trees (West Indian plums, ginip, papaya and several others) were plentiful. While the islands lacked big game, farm-raised agouti, birds, eggs and reptiles provided a culinary variety. Often a pot could be found simmering on the village fire. Villagers would dip into the pot when hungry and augment the pot with additional food as needed.

* *

And so it was before the moment of discovery by Columbus on Friday the 12th of 1492.

As the explorers "from the sky" stepped forth on the paradise islands, the simple lives of the Caribbean Indians would change forever.

Who could have predicted the destiny of despair and extinction that would befall these beautiful people at this historic moment?

* *

Readers interested in what followed this "new world" discovery may wish to read, "A Brief History of the Caribbean: From the Arawak and Caribs to the Present," written by Jan Rogonzinski, "Columbus - the Four Voyages" by Laurence Bergreen and "Columbus the Discoverer," by Frederick Ober.

Footnote:

Marie-Galante (named Aichi by the Caribs and *Touloukaera* by the Tainos) was inhabited by Caribs at the time Columbus discovered the new world in 1492. As a small island, it clearly lacked the resources to sustain a large resident population. The island families and clans lived in small villages most likely on the southern shore near today's Grand-Bourg and near the freshwaters at St-Louis and Vieux-Fort. Like the Tainos, they were skilled fishermen, excellent sailors and agriculturists.

On November 3, 1493 during his second trip, Columbus stopped at Marie-Galante and named this inviting speck of land after "Santa Marie la Galante" his flagship.

Several of his men experimented with the apple-like fruit of the poisonous manchineel tree located on Marie-Galante's beaches. Columbus records that their faces swelled and they became violently sick with symptom of rabies.

Two hours after tasting this fruit, their tongues afire, plus a hostile welcome from native Caribs, Columbus and his band of mariners departed in search of friendlier places.

Concept of Native Caribbean Village at the time of Columbus. Courtesy Abigail M. Frederick, Artist.

APPENDICES

1. **Phrases English to French**

2. **Highway Signs**

3. **Currency**

4. **Ten Reasons Why People Like The Beach**

5. **Beach Quest**

6. **The Myth of Ayacayia**

7. **Beach Anatomy**

8. **Poetry**

9. **Did You Know?**

10. **References**

1. PHRASES ENGLISH TO FRENCH

ENGLISH	PRONUNCIATION	FRENCH
Do you speak English?	Par-lay voo ahn-glay	Parlez-vous anglais?
Excuse me/sorry	Ex-koo-zay mwah	Excusez-moi
Fine thanks and you?	Bee-ehn mer-see ay voo?	Bien merci, et vous?
Good-by	Oh ruh-vwar	Au revoir
Good evening	Bawn-swar	Bon soir
Good morning/good day	Bawn-zhoor	Bon jour
Hello	Sah-loo	Salut
Here	Ee-see	Ici
How are you?	Kom-mohn tah-lay voo	Comment allez-vous?
I don't understand	Jhuhn kom-prohn pah	Je ne comprends pas
I'm sorry	Day-zoh-lay/pahr-dohn	Desolé/Pardon
My name is	Juh mah-pell	Je m'appelle
No	Nohn	Non
Ok	Dah-core	D'accord
Pardon me	Pahr-dohn	Pardon
Please	Seel voo play	S'il vous plaît
Pleased to meet you	Ohn--shahn-tay	Enchanté(e)
Please speak slowly	Par-lay lehn-ta-mohn	Parlez lentement
So-so	Kum-see, kum-sah	Comme ci, comme ça
Thank you	Mare-see	Merci
That's ok	Dah ree-ehn	De rien
There	Lah	Là
Very well	Treh bee-ehn	Très bien

ENGLISH	PRONUNCIATION	FRENCH
What?	Kom-mohn	Comment?
I would like	(jeuh v00-dray	Je voudrais
How much?	(cawm-byen)	Combien
Where is the restroom?	(ooway la twah-let)	Où est la toilette?
When	Kohn	Quand
Where	Oo	Où
You' re welcome	Dah ree-**ehn**	De rien
Beer, dark	Lah bee-**yehr** brewn	La bièr brune
Coffee with cream	Leh ka-**fay** krem	Le café crème
Orange juice	Leh juj doh-**rahnzj**	Le jus d'orange
Bread	Banhh	Bain
Butter	Bearre	Beurre
Eggs	Oeffe	Oeuf
Supermarket	Leh sue-pehr-mahr-**shay**	Le Supermarché
Breakfast	Leh Puh-Tee Day-Zhuh- **Nay**	Le Petit-Déjeuner
Dinner	leh dee-nay	le dîner
Lunch	leh day-zhun-nay	le déjeuner
Grocery	Lay-pees-ree	L'épicerie
Wine, white	Leh vohn blohn	Le vin blanc
The	Laa/Leh	La/Lẻ
Can you help me?	Pu va-vu made e?	Po Pouvez-vous m'aider?
a	un/in	Un/une

	This symbol identifies scenic overlooks and parking spaces. If you are not in a hurry, this is a good spot to stop, take a photo, have a snack, stretch legs and check out your map location. You may have to walk down a path to see the panorama overview of the countryside, scenic valley or historic site. Some sites have an orientation map showing points of interest.
	This sign means you are coming to a junction of a minor crossroad. You have priority.
	If the triangle has an "x" it means you are coming to a junction where traffic on the right has priority– give way to the right.
	This symbol is usually seen on a main road as you leave a town or village. It means that you are on a "route prioritaire" (priority route) and have priority over drivers on intersecting roads. All traffic joining from side roads must give way. These signs are repeated at frequent intervals along the priority route.
	A diagonal slash through the priority route symbol ends the priority zone. Drivers from the right have priority unless there are road signs or markings indicating otherwise.

	Stop really does mean stop. These are commonly used to slow (calm) traffic. They may appear in places where a "give way sign" would be more appropriate, or where logic would dictate that you would normally have priority over a side road. When approaching these signs you should stop and come to a complete halt before moving on.
	An isosceles triangle pointing downward means you must give way to traffic on the major road.
	This denotes a one-way street. Do not enter.
	This is not a route sign; it is a speed limit sign showing the maximum allowable speed in kilometers/hr.
	Blue and red sign indicates you are entering a "No Parking" or "No Waiting Zone." The same circle in black and white with a bar through it indicates you're leaving the no parking zone.

	A circle with an arrow in it shows the direction that all traffic must follow. If it points right you must turn right.
	Circular arrows in an isosceles triangle indicate that you are entering a roundabout; stay right; yield to all traffic in the circle.
	This symbol indicates a pedestrian crossing ahead.

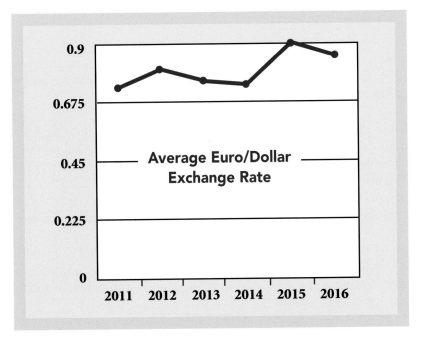

For today's exchange rate and a currency converter visit XE.com.

Euros are used for currency in the French West Indies. For the better part of a decade, 1 dollar would buy you less than 0.8 Euros. While the exchange rate averaged around 0.8, a record high exchange rate of 1 US Dollar to 1.0098 Euros occurred on November 28, 2002 while the record lowest rate occurred on November 10, 2007 when the Dollar purchased 0.68 Euros. Similar exchange rate fluctuation exists for the British Pound and other currencies. A visit to XE.com provides up-to-date conversion information.

The US Dollar and Euro are approaching parity again. The strengthening of the Dollar is good news for both tourists who have extra Dollars to spend on "good deals" (wine, food, entertainment, etc.) and for Marie-Galante's businesses who benefit from stepped up spending.

For travel money, you will need to go to your local bank and request a conversion of Dollars to Euros. The banks don't keep a stash of Euros so make your request 2 to 3 weeks before trip departure so they can go to their central source to acquire the right amount. The Euro is issued in paper denominations of £5, £10, £20, £50, £100, £200, and £500. Euro coins are issued in denominations of £0.01, £0.02, £0.05, £0.10, £0.20, £0.50, £1, and £2.

Credit cards are accepted at many restaurants, car rentals and other businesses. Visa and MasterCard are widely accepted, but most merchants do not accept American Express or Discover cards.

If you use credit cards and pay your biggest expenses (air fare and villa rentals) ahead of time, there is no need to carry large amounts of cash. Plan for out-of-pocket expenses in Euros for taxis and ferry costs (buy a round trip ferry ticket unless you plan on a permanent stay on this paradise island). Keep Euros handy for excursions, parking (don't forget the parking fee to exit the airport lot when you get home) and small business purchases where a credit card is not accepted.

There are ATM machines (called ABMs or distributors des billets) on the island if you run a little short. Don't forget to set up the PIN number at your home town bank before leaving home. This will take a few days, so plan to obtain a PIN a week ahead of your departure.

When converting Dollars to Euros many banks will charge a transaction fee. An exception to this fee is the Bank of America which will convert Dollars to Euros at no costs to their customers.

Likewise, some credit cards impose a transaction fee for credit card charges in Euros. Bank of America also offers a credit card which will convert Euros to Dollars at the daily rate without the surcharge fee.

4. TEN REASONS WHY PEOPLE LIKE THE BEACH

(David Letterman Order)

. . . .

I like the fact my whole family is together at one time in one place. I love the smiles on the children as they play in the water. I love talking to my family into the wee hours of the night. The beach is about memories which carry us through the years. T.B. Whitt, Author

10. FOR CHILDREN OF ALL TIME

To the question, a 20 month old child replied when asked about fun at the beach; Wet..... Bucket..... Digger....Digger....Mommy.

9. YOU'RE LESS LIKELY TO DIE

A study of 12,000 men showed that those who didn't take an annual holiday were 32% more likely to die of a heart attack. Choose life. Choose the beach.

8. CARIBBEAN HIGH

The awesome beauty of the emerald world of Marie-Galante is breathtaking, inspirational and romantic. Share it with your lover. A moonlight walk among the stars of the universe and the glow of the Caribbean Sea provides a romance experience found nowhere else in the world!

7. READING IS RESTFUL

Research shows that simply reading for pleasure reduces stress by 68%. What's more, this improved mood can be seen in a mere 6 minutes. Imagine how de-stressed (and happy) you would be after two weeks at the beach.

Everyone packs a book in their beach bag.
"A beach without a book is like a flirt without a look."

6. THE OCEAN WATER IS HEALTHFUL

Taking a dip at the beach opens the pores and helps to remove toxins from your body, plus there's enough magnesium in the water to have a significant effect on calming one's nerves. Also, the ultraviolet rays in sunshine improve your sense of physical and emotional well-being by stimulating the production of vitamin D. This boosts production of serotonin, the chemical that raises alertness, optimism and happiness.

5. BE LAZY - THERE IS NO RACE TODAY

Do nothing. Sunbathe. Take a nap. It helps to reduce blood pressure and prolong life. Cats know that. They have 9 lives.

Throughout humanity, man's instincts have led him to the beach to seek the perfect 20 minute nap. That nap is lying on a beach blanket under the warmth of the sun at high noon. Research shows that the sound of waves alters the wave patterns in the brain, making you more calm and relaxed. Falling asleep to the sound of crashing waves or the gentle lapping of the waves brings about a blissful calmness and happiness.

4. LET'S HAVE A PARTY

Playing Frisbee, riding the waves on a boogie board, diving into the breakers and playing volley ball is fun when you are with your family and friends. Have you had a beach party lately?

3. A BEACH IS FOR EXPLORATION

The beach is an explorer's paradise. Above water, a search for the intimate cove awaits discovery. Waves bring in treasures for the beachcomber -- shells, weathered glass and driftwood.

A biological landscape awaits the naturalist. Snorkeling reveals an underwater kaleidoscope of color and marine diversity. Tropical Fish of unusual shape and behavior abound.

2. PICNICKING IS FUN

There is nothing like a picnic basket full of snacks, a wedge of cheese, a crust of French bread and a glass of wine. Or as Norm would say:

"Nothing beats the feeling of freedom that accompanies a lunch-time beer — Just because you can." Attributed to Norm of Cheers

1. AND THE NUMBER ONE REASON PEOPLE GO TO THE BEACH IS — *A BEACH IS A PLACE FOR LOVE*

Sometimes the ultimate wisdom on the great questions of life can be found with family, boyfriend, girlfriend and soul-mates. People go to the beach with someone they love. In fact, beaches are so good for love vibes that 46% of honeymooners head to one to celebrate their nuptials. Say I love you in French. "Je t'aime."

5. BEACH QUEST

People of all ages enjoy beach hunting, whether they are looking for shells in the sand or fish in the water, they enjoy exploring the beaches of Marie-Galante. So if you're looking for a whimsical way to pass the day, consider this entertaining beach quest. Check them off as you discover them.

☐ 1. Two different kinds of shells (e.g. coiled snail, bi-valve clam)

☐ 2. A limpet shell (with a hole in top)

☐ 3. A unique piece of driftwood

☐ 4. A creature's home

☐ 5. Something swimming in the water. What is it?

☐ 6. Soft coral (e.g. sea fan) and stone coral (e.g. brain coral)

☐ 7. Build a sand castle. Take a picture

☐ 8. Five different colored stones

☐ 9. Sea grapes

☐ 10. Three pieces of trash. Identify. (Pick up and place in trash can)

☐ 11. Three pieces of sea glass (different colors)

☐ 12. Sargasso (algae with tooth-edged leaves with no holdfast)

☐ 13. An animal track in the sand. What animal made the track?

☐ 14. A cloud animal or castle. What do you see?

☐ 15. Fishing tackle (net, lure or line)

☐ 16. How many waves crash into shore in one minute?

☐ 17. How many paces wide is the beach?

☐ 18. Identify unusual things (e.g. cairn, turtle). Take pictures

☐ 19. Wade into the water. How much time for your feet to dry?

☐ 20. Smile at ten people. How many smile back?

Mermaid of the Caribbean Sea

Legend has it that long ago the men on a beautiful Caribbean island had become lazy drunkards, unfaithful to their wives and unwilling to hunt and fish for their families. The island chief, eager to remedy these evils and restore moral values, went seeking guidance from the ancestral spirits known to reside in a sacred grove of trees. Upon explaining the problem the spirits said;

"These evils are caused by seven sisters who sing seductive songs and perform sensual dances. So enchanting and beautiful are these women that they rob men of free will."

To restore order in the village, the chief decided that the seven women should be killed. When the moment of execution came, the chief, taken by their beauty, changed his mind and banished them instead to the island of Jagua located far, far away.

And so the women were placed in a canoe and with the strongest oarsmen of the island, embarked on a journey to the island of Jagua. In the middle of their journey the oarsmen realized that they had only six sisters. Aycayia the most beautiful of all was missing.

As they began to turn back to find Aycayia the winds began to blow with such great force that the canoe capsized drowning all on board.

Aycayia who had been warned of plans for her exile had remained back to entertain the men with her sensuous dance and sweet and melodious voice. Throughout the island men were spellbound by her beauty and sexually generous seductions, turning them from work, luring them from their wives and destroying island harmony.

There came a time when the chief sought help a second time in the wooded grove of the ancestral spirits. Upon explaining the difficulty that the chief faced, the great spirits spoke;

"Aycayia embodies sin - the sin of beauty, art and love.
She provides men pleasure and makes them her slaves, stealing their will.
And her diabolical strength is that satisfying each man with her charm,
she delivers none to all. If you want to live in peace, you must be brave
in your heart and exile her for eternity."

And so the chief condemned Aycayia to live a lonely life with an old woman on a distant and secret island. But men soon found her place of exile and visited her to see her beauty, watch her seductive dance and hear her sweet and caressing voice. As before, the beauty and power of Aycayia was strong and she soon created an empire over all, robbing men of their free will.

So the chief sought help from the ancestral spirits a third time and the great spirits said;

"Here is a sack of small black seeds. These seeds are an amulet that
will break the spell of Aycayia and restore the free will of all men.
Affection and fidelity between man and wife will return.
Tranquility and peace will again exist throughout the land."

"Deliver these seeds to the women on your island who must carefully plant and nourish each. One seed will give rise to a tree that will go by the name of Majagua. When grown, the leaves, flowers and bark will break the spell of enchantment, releasing all men from Aycayia's power."

The seeds were carefully planted and soon grew to trees of great beauty. As a beautiful flower on the most magnificent tree bloomed, there came a violent hurricane with raging waves never seen before. And with these raging waves, Aycayia and her sins of beauty, art and love were dragged out to the waters deep.

And it came to pass, to the waters deep, Aycayia grew fins by which to swim and gills by which to breathe. There she lives eternally dancing seductively in the waves, singing her sweet song to the winds and beckoning men to leave their boat to be with her at sea. And the old woman you may ask, what happened to her? Why she lives with Aycayia in a coral kingdom as a green turtle.

7. BEACH ANATOMY

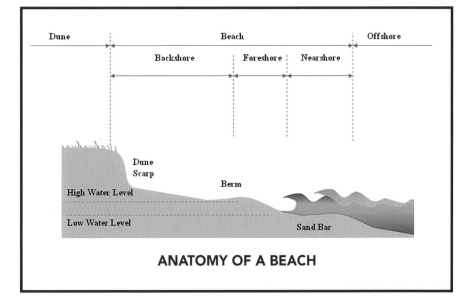

ANATOMY OF A BEACH

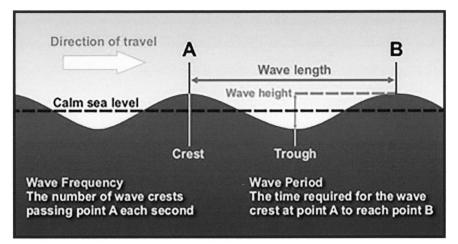

Courtesy: NOAA's National Ocean Services Education

Beaches encompass the area from the reef where large ocean waves are transformed from large to small and the high water mark on the back shore of storm surges. The active beach may be a few hundred feet or a half mile or more. Beaches are composed of three parts; 1) a backshore (that portion of the beach upland of the berm); 2) a foreshore (the active area that is constantly washed by the incoming waves; and 3) the nearshore (the underwater zone where beach waves are formed).

High waves with short periods cause the beach to erode and the berm to shift to an underwater sand bar. Lower waves with longer periods cause sand from the bar to move the berm.

Wave height is determined by wind speed, wind duration and fetch (the distance over water that the wind blows in a single direction. If the wind is weak, small waves form. If the wind is strong but only lasts a few minutes, only small waves form. If strong winds blow for a long period over a short fetch, then only small waves are formed. When all three exist (strong winds, for an extended time, over a long fetch, then large waves form. (Duxbury, et al, 2002).

The constant gentle breeze and the offshore reefs protect Marie-Galante's eastern beaches. On the leeward western shore the island itself shelters the beach. Conditions are just right for the formation of many enduring and beautiful beaches — protected beaches that are not eroded by destructive waves and other eroding forces.

8. POETRY

Elegy Written
In A Country Clock Factory

By Robert A. Sausville

Time; old and yet a most relentless foe.
Your enemies must falter one by one.
They pause to fight but briefly, then must go,
Like shadows dying swiftly in the sun.

The worldly gains of human enterprise,
The goals attained through constant toil and strife,
Erode with measured beat before your eyes
And fall as grain before the reapers knife.

The gentle ticking of a friendly clock
In soothing comfort to the homely room.
Our dreams and hopes not only does it mock
But echoes forth a grim forecast of doom.

Like steps resounding from the pavement stone
The seconds mark our progress on the road.
Each hour another milepost they intone
A parting knell to this our brief abode.

Plod on you demon of the fruitless years
Engulfing all within your mystic realm
The ship of life but fleetingly appears
And time directs the movement of the helm.

If on this cruise I sail the stormy seas
Don't think that I will not enjoy the ride,
For rum and fare I'll gladly pay the fees
And let you choose the landing; reef or tide.

Beachcomber

By Robert Service

When I have come with happy heart to sixty years and ten,
I'll buy a boat and sail away upon a summer sea;
And in a little lonely isle that's far and far from men,
In peace and praise I'll spend the days the gods allow to me.
For I am weary of a strife so pitiless and vain;
And in a far and fairy isle, bewilderingly bright,
I'll learn to know the leap and glow of rapture once again,
And welcome every living dawn with wonder and delight.

And there I'll build a swan-white house above the singing foam,
With brooding eaves, where joyously rich roses climb and cling;
With crotons in a double row, like wine and honeycomb,
And flame trees dripping golden rain, and palms pavilioning.
And there I'll let the wind and waves do their will with me;
And I will dwell unto the end with loveliness and joy;
And drink from all the crystal springs and eat from off the trees,
As simple as a savage is, as careless as a boy.

For I have come to think that life's a lamentable tale,
And all we break our hearts to win is little worth our while;
For fame and fortune in the end are comfortless and stale,
And it is best to dream and rest upon a radiant isle.
So I'll blot out the bitter years of sufferance and scorn,
And I'll forget the fear and fret, the poverty and pain;
And in a shy and secret isle I'll be a man newborn,
And fashion life to heart's desire, and seek my soul again.

For when I come with happy heart to sixty years and ten,
I fondly hope the best of life will yet remain to me;
And so I'll burn my foolish books and break my futile pen,
And seek a quiet tranquil isle, that dreams eternally.
I'll turn my back on all the world, I'll bid my friends adieu;
Unto the blink I'll leave behind what gold I have to give;
And in a jeweled solitude I'll mould my life anew,
And nestling close to nature's heart, I'll learn at last . . . to live.

9. DID YOU KNOW?

1. **Island Population** - In 1946, the population of Marie-Galante was 30,000. Today, the population is 12,009. Grand-Bourg's population is 5707, Capesterre 3469 and St-Louis 2833. Population loss is due to a decline in sugar cane farming.

2. **Turtle Sex** - Beach forests are important nesting sites for hawksbill turtles. Nests in the cooler forests produce male turtles; those on the sunny beaches produce females. Unless the beach forests are protected, there may not be enough male hawksbill turtles to maintain a stable population.

3. **Hard Shells/Soft Shells** - Most shells found on the beach are marine mollusks, partly because many of these shells endure better than softer seashells which exist on barnacles, crabs, lobsters and brachiopods.

4. **Island Temperature** - Marie-Galante's average monthly temperature varies by only 3° C (5° F) year-round. This is due to the favorable trade winds (les alizés), which bring refreshing breezes from the northeast throughout the year. Average air temperatures on the coast range from 22° to 30° C (72° to 86° F). Inland, temperatures vary from 19° to 27° C (66° to 81° F). The warm coastal water temperatures stay between 26.7° and 29.4° C (80° and 85° F).

5. **Size of Island** - Marie-Galante has a land area of 170.5 km² (61 sq. miles). Its diameter is about 10 miles. Because the island is round and flat, it is sometimes referred to as "La grande galette" (the big pancake). The island has rolling hills, with a maximum elevation of 670 feet (204 meters) above sea level.

6. **Tidal Variation** -The difference between high and low tide on the island is a maximum of 1.6 feet (0.49 meters), thus washout of the beaches does not normally occur. Tidal differences along the Maine coast are 20 feet (6.1 meters).

7. **Survival at Sea** - In 1982 Steve Callahan survived 76 days as he drifted 1,800 perilous miles across the Atlantic in a rubber raft, battling starvation, thirst, sharks and storms. He was discovered and rescued off the coast of Marie-Galante by local fishermen. He recounts his experience in the book entitled "Adrift."

8. **Underwater Pressure** - For every 33 feet (10.06 meters) of depth, the pressure increases by 14.5 psi. In the deepest ocean, the pressure is equivalent to the weight of an elephant balanced on a postage stamp.

9. **Underwater Sound** - Pressure in the deep sections of the ocean increases the speed of underwater sound. In these depths, sound can travel thousands of miles. In fact, hydrophones (underwater microphones), if placed at the proper depth, can pick up whale songs and manmade noises over 12 miles away.

10. **Longevity of Whales** - Whales are the largest mammal on earth and the longest living mammal too. According to scientists, a colossal Bowhead whale, a year-round Arctic dweller, may live 200-plus years.

11. **Sargassum** - The Sargasso Sea is a vast patch of free-floating seaweed called Sargassum. Sargassum provides a home to an amazing variety of marine species. Turtles use sargassum mats as nurseries where hatchlings have food and shelter. Sargassum also provides essential habitat for shrimp, crab, fish, and other marine species that have adapted specifically to this floating vegetation. Recently mats of Sargassum have washed on to the shores of Caribbean islands to the displeasure of tourists.

12. **Mangroves** -There are about 80 different species of mangrove trees. All of these trees grow in low-oxygen soil where slow-moving water allows fine sediments to accumulate. Mangrove forests only grow at tropical and subtropical latitudes near the equator because they cannot withstand freezing temperatures. Mangrove forests stabilize the coastline, reducing erosion from storm surges, currents, waves, and tides. The intricate root system of mangroves also makes these forests attractive to fish and other organisms seeking food and shelter from predators. Long mangrove roots have the unique ability to take up salt water and transform it to fresh water.

13. **West Indies** - The term West Indies usually refers to the non-Latin islands of the Caribbean. After Christopher Columbus's first voyage to the Americas, Europeans began to use the term West Indies to differentiate the newly discovered Caribbean islands from islands in South and Southeast Asia. Those islands that are under the jurisdiction of France are referred to as the French West Indies.

14. **Greater Antilles** - This refers to a group of large islands in the West Indies that include Cuba, Hispaniola (Haiti and Dominican Republic), Jamaica, & Puerto Rico.

15. **Lesser Antilles** - The islands of the Lesser Antilles consist of the smaller islands not listed as part of the Greater Antilles. They include Windward Islands in the south (south of Dominica) the Leeward Islands in the north. The Windward Islands are so called because they were more windward (downwind) to sailing ships arriving in the New World than the Leeward Islands, given that the prevailing trade winds blow east to west. Marie-Galante is a Leeward Island in the Lesser Antilles.

16. **Baby Powder** - To remove sand sticking to you feet or backpack rub a small amount of powder over the sandy area.

17. **Rollers (Ground Seas)** - Large ocean swells which occur in calm weather without obvious cause are called ground seas. They result in large waves (rollers) which break with a roar on the reefs or shore.

18. **Caribbean Sea** - Between South and Central America and the chain of islands on the east (the Greater and Lesser Antilles) lies the Caribbean Sea. With an area of nearly 1.1 million square miles, it is one of the largest seas on earth.

10. REFERENCES

1. *Beachcombing at Miramar,* Richard Bade, 1996.

2. *IGN Map - Saint-Francois,Marie-Galante,* LaDesirade, 2015.

3. *A Brief History of the Caribbean,* Jan Rogozinski, 1999.

4. *St. John, Feet, Fins and Four-wheel Drive,* Pam Gaffin, 1994.

5. *Voyage of the Turtle,* Carl Safina, 2006.

6. *Humorous Verse,* Robert A. Sausville, 2015.

7. *Fishes of the Caribbean Reefs,* Ian F. Took, 1982.

8. *Atlantic Coast Beaches,* William J. Neal, Orrin H. Pilkey and Joseph T. Kelley, 2007.

9. *Flowers of the Caribbean,* G. W. Lennox and S.A. Seddon, 2014.

10. *National Geographic Field Guide to the Water's Edge,* Stephen Leatherman and Jack Williams.

11. *The Naturalist Guide To the Atlantic Seashore,* Scott W. Shumway, 2008.

12. *Insight Guide to Thailand's Beaches and Islands,* 2012.

13. *Reef Fish Identification,* Paul Humann and Ned Deloach, 2014.

14. *Indigenous People of the Caribbean,* Samuel M. Wilson, 1997.

15. *Columbus* - The Four Voyages, Lawrence Bergreen, 2011.

16. *Snorkeling - A Complete Guide to the Underwater Experience,* John R. Clark, 1995.

17. *Eastern Caribbean,* Lonely Planet, 2001.

18. *Florida's Living beaches,* Blair and Dawn Witherington, 2007

19. *St. John - Off the Beaten Track,* Gerald Singer, 2016.

20. *Sea Turtles, A Complete Guide to Their Biology, Behavior and Conservation,* James R. Spotilla, 2004

21. *Sea Turtles, An Extraordinary Natural History of Some Uncommon Turtles,* Blair Witherington, 2006

22. *A Beachcombers Odyssey,* S. Decon Rittyerbush, PhD, 2008

23. *Leeward Anchorages,* Cruising Guide Publications, Chris Doyle, 2010

24. *Guadeloupe, Marie-Galante and Saintes Islands; Discover A Caribbean Paradise!* 2016 Cristina Rebiere and Olivier Rebiere

NOTES

NOTES

NOTES